Casey at the Bat

LeRoy Neiman

LeRoy Neiman

Casey at the Bat

Ernest Lawrence Thayer

Introduction by Joe Torre

ecco

An Imprint of HarperCollinsPublishers

INTRODUCTION
by Joe Torre

I've been thinking about why young boys and girls should read *Casey at the Bat.* Of course there's the excitement and expectation, which are part of the fabric of the game. But more important, it's a story about our ability to deal with what appears to be failure. The poem makes clear that it's not possible to succeed every time at the plate—or every day at whatever you do in life. Reading *Casey at the Bat* allows you a little more patience with yourself and with others.

Even though we may feel that Casey let us down, I don't believe our opinion of him as a player is really any different than if he'd hit that home run. This is something I tell my players. If Derek Jeter strikes out in a critical situation, am I disappointed in him? No, I'm not. You have to bring common sense to the game, which is easy for me to do because I'm not the one throwing the bat, feeling like I've let everybody down.

It's the same whether you're playing sandlot ball or at Yankee Stadium: There's a winner and there's a loser, exhilaration and misery. There's no greater feeling of satisfaction than winning and no lower feeling than losing. But it may be that remembering how you feel when you win keeps you from staying down when you're defeated. It's important for players to understand, "Hey, I didn't *lose,* he *beat* me this time." You've got to tip your hat to the other guy once in a while.

Striking out is as difficult for the pros as it is for Little Leaguers. It's perceived as failure, especially when a game is in the balance, as it was for Casey. I need to remind my players of all they've accomplished. What makes a good player is the capacity to forget the last at bat.

Although certain aspects of baseball have changed over the years, the one thing that has *not* changed—and part of the message of *Casey at the Bat*—is that it's still the *playing* of the game that counts. When all is said and done, you still put on your uniform, lace up your shoes, and get between the lines, where you're on your own.

When I read *Casey at the Bat* I visualize a Babe Ruth–type guy with a potbelly. But LeRoy Neiman's Casey has just come from the gym, which makes him a contemporary ballplayer—muscles rippling under his shirt. Still, I would choose a Mariano Rivera over a teamful of Caseys. There have been only a handful of batters who have hit .400, and even they fail six times out of ten. The pitcher always has the advantage. I remember watching Pedro Martinez pitch when I managed an

American League All-Star team. You had Mark McGwire and Sammy Sosa at the plate, and I thought to myself, "They won't even foul tip a ball off Martinez—you don't make a living hitting off Pedro Martinez." The axiom has always been and will always be: Good pitching stops good hitting.

There's serious nonverbal communication going on between a batter and a pitcher. It's all body language. I used to watch Bob Gibson on the mound, and he would intimidate me with a scowl; Roger Clemens too is good at that, as is Pedro Martinez. Something else that comes into play in this duel is the art of throwing close to hitters. Back in the years when I played, if a pitcher hit you, he never let on if it was intentional. This makes batters uneasy. And that's part of what any good pitcher needs to have going for him—an air of mystery.

A home run hitter has his own body language. He displays a confidence that says, "I'm going to make you throw the ball over the plate and I'm going to deposit it somewhere very far away." This kind of bravado translates through the body, and all the great home run hitters I've known have had it—as does LeRoy's Casey.

The home run is a very American thing. It's what kids in the backyard do—and it's what I did growing up. You hit a home run in the ninth inning of the last game of the World Series and you trot around what you imagine are the bases. But the home run is exactly what I try to have my players *not* think about. Even though it's the home run that turns people on, it doesn't work for the team, because it focuses too much on the individual. I like the home run to be a surprise rather than something we hold our breath for.

If you get excited about the home run, you have to accept the strikeout, which can be as sensational as the home run—and aside from DiMaggio, home run hitters strike out a lot. When someone like Casey or Babe Ruth or Mark McGwire swings, it's an ear-shattering sound: the swing and the miss. People complain that baseball moves too slowly. But I believe there's no more spellbinding confrontation than that between the pitcher and the batter. It's truly exciting—it's what baseball's all about.

Ultimately, *Casey at the Bat* is whatever you want it to be, a game of ball or a confrontation emblematic of life. But for me it comes down to something simple—putting in a good day's work and being satisfied with the fact that you've taken part in something very special. LeRoy places great passion into the faces of the players, as well as the crowd. He looks into their eyes and draws what he finds there. He puts a face and personality on this sport, which has become so impersonal. And he understands the passion that from time to time can be a part of *our* lives.

The outlook wasn't brilliant

The score stood four to

And then when Cooney died at

A sickly silence fell upon

for the Mudville nine that day;

two with but one inning more to play.

second, and Burrows did the same,

the patrons of the game.

A straggling few got up

The rest clung to the hope which

They thought, "If only Casey

We'd put up even money

to go in deep despair.

springs eternal in the human breast;

could but get a whack at that —

now with Casey at the bat."

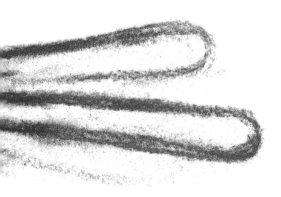

But Flynn preceded Casey,
    as did also Jimmy Blake,
And the former was a lulu
    and the latter was a fake;
So upon that stricken multitude
    a deathlike silence sat,
For there seemed but little chance
    of Casey's getting to the bat.

But Flynn let drive a single,

to the wonderment of all,

And Blake, the much despis-ed,

        tore the cover off the ball;

And when the dust had lifted,

There was Jimmy safe

and the men saw what had occurred,

at second and Flynn a-hugging third.

Then from five thousand throats

It rumbled in the

It knocked upon the hillside

and more there rose a lusty yell;

mountaintops, it rattled in the dell;

and recoiled upon the flat,

For Casey, mighty Casey,

was advancing to the bat.

There was ease in Casey's manner

as he stepped into his place;

There was pride in Casey's bearing

and a smile on Casey's face.

And when, responding to the cheers,

he lightly doffed his hat,

No stranger in the crowd

could doubt 'twas Casey at the bat.

Ten thousand eyes were on him

as he rubbed his hands with dirt;

Five thousand tongues applauded

when he wiped them on his shirt.

Then while the writhing pitcher

      ground the ball into his hip,

Defiance gleamed in Casey's eye,
a sneer curled Casey's lip.

And now the leather-covered sphere

came hurtling through the air,

And Casey stood a-watching it

in haughty grandeur there.

Close by the sturdy batsman the ball

unheeded sped —

"That ain't my style," said Casey.

"Strike one," the umpire said.

From the benches, black with

Like the beating of the storm-waves

"Kill him! Kill the umpire!"

people, there went up a muffled roar,

on a stern and distant shore.

houted someone on the stand;

And it's likely they'd have killed him

had not Casey raised his hand.

With a smile of Christian charity

    great Casey's visage shone;

He stilled the rising tumult;

    he bade the game go on;

He signaled to the pitcher,

and once more the spheroid flew;

But Casey still ignored it,

and the umpire said, "Strike two."

"Fraud!" cried the maddened thousands,

and the echo answered, "Fraud!"

But one scornful look from Casey
and the multitude was awed.
They saw his face grow stern and cold,
they saw his muscles strain,

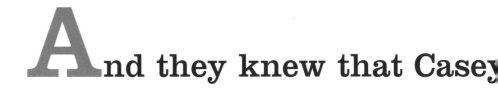

wouldn't let that ball go by again.

The sneer is gone from Casey's lip,

    his teeth are clenched in hate;

He pounds with cruel violence

    his bat upon the plate.

And now the pitcher holds the ball,

and now he lets it go,

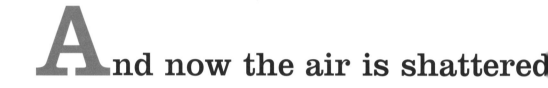And now the air is shattered

by the force of Casey's blow.

Oh, somewhere in this

The band is playing somewhere,

And somewhere men are

favored land the sun is shining bright;

and somewhere hearts are light,

laughing, and somewhere children shout;

But there is no joy in Mudville —

mighty Casey has struck out.

Originally published by Deuce II Editions, New York, 2000.

CASEY AT THE BAT. Illustrations copyright © 2000 by LeRoy Neiman. Compilation copyright © 2000 by Deuce II Editions. Introduction © 2002 by Joe Torre. All rights reserved. Printed in Singapore. No part of this book may be used or reproduced in any manner whatsoever without written permission except in the case of brief quotations embodied in critical articles and reviews. For information address HarperCollins Publishers Inc., 10 East 53rd Street, New York, NY 10022.

HarperCollins books may be purchased for educational, business, or sales promotional use. For information please write: Special Markets Department, HarperCollins Publishers Inc., 10 East 53rd Street, New York, NY 10022.

First Ecco edition June 2002.

Designed by Katy Homans.

The type is Clarendon.

Library of Congress Cataloging-in-Publication Data has been applied for.

ISBN 0-06-009068-5

02 03 04 05 06 TWP 10 9 8 7 6 5 4 3 2 1

making DIVERSITY WORK

7 STEPS for DEFEATING BIAS in the WORKPLACE

SONDRA THIEDERMAN, PH.D.

Dearborn™
Trade Publishing
A **Kaplan Professional** Company

This publication is designed to provide accurate and authoritative information in regard to the subject matter covered. It is sold with the understanding that the publisher is not engaged in rendering legal, accounting, or other professional service. If legal advice or other expert assistance is required, the services of a competent professional person should be sought.

Vice President and Publisher: Cynthia A. Zigmund
Acquisitions Editor: Jonathan Malysiak
Senior Managing Editor: Jack Kiburz
Interior Design: Lucy Jenkins
Cover Design: Jody Billert, Billert Communications
Typesetting: the dotted i

Published by Dearborn Trade Publishing
A Kaplan Professional Company

Printed in the United States of America

03   04   05   10 9 8 7 6 5 4 3 2 1

Library of Congress Cataloging-in-Publication Data

Thiederman, Sondra B.
    Making diversity work : seven steps for defeating bias in the workplace / Sondra Thiederman.
        p.   cm.
    Includes index.
    ISBN 0-7931-7763-4 (6x9 hardcover)
    1. Discrimination in employment.   I. Title: Seven steps for defeating bias in the workplace.   II. Title.
HD4903.T48 2003
658.3'008—dc21

2003007493

Dearborn Trade books are available at special quantity discounts to use for sales promotions, employee premiums, or educational purposes. Please call our Special Sales Department to order or for more information at 800-245-2665, e-mail trade@dearborn.com, or write to Dearborn Trade Publishing, 30 South Wacker Drive, Suite 2500, Chicago, IL 60606-7481.

Advance Praise for *Making Diversity Work*

"Sondra Thiederman's new book effectively examines the thorniest prejudices that exist around race, gender, and other dimensions of human difference. This book, *Making Diversity Work,* is an important addition to the field in that it provides tools that enable individuals to become immediate problem solvers in this vital area. As such, it will be indispensable to any thoughtful person seeking a fresh and innovative framework for tackling the challenge of workplace bias."

—Dr. R. Roosevelt Thomas, Jr., President and CEO, Roosevelt Thomas Consulting and Training

"*Making Diversity Work* is a slam-dunk winner. It addresses a challenge that is as big an issue in the world of basketball as in the workplace: How can we rid ourselves of the biases that interfere with our ability to build winning teams? Sondra Thiederman's play-by-play strategy for reducing bias is essential for anyone who is serious about making diversity work in their organization."

—Bill Walton, NBA Legend, ABC and ESPN Basketball Analyst

"Finally, a business approach to workplace diversity! Having been exposed to Sondra's unique perspective when she addressed our management team, I am not surprised to discover that she has written a book which talks about diversity in a way that makes good business sense. She clearly recognizes that bias reduction is more than just a 'feel good' issue."

—Pattye Moore, President, Sonic Corporation

"*Making Diversity Work* is an excellent field guide for leveraging the power of diversity in any business. Dr. Thiederman provides real-world illustrations of the often subtle biases held by us all. She then takes the next critical step of outlining how those perceptions negatively impact people and, by extension, business. This book should be required reading for any organization committed to leveraging the power of diversity."

—Jo Jerman, Vice President, Southeast Business Group, Merck & Company, Inc.

"Dr. Sondra Thiederman's book is an urgent reminder of why making diversity work remains America's great challenge. As long as bias remains a palpable presence in the workplace, important promises of the world's leading democratic society will remain unfulfilled. Her book is highly readable and filled with useable and practical strategies to overcome bias. It is a must read for everyone interested in attaining a level playing field."

—Price M. Cobbs, M.D., President and CEO, Pacific Management Systems

"Sondra Thiederman must be applauded for breaking new ground in the treatment of an old subject that continues to be a barrier to achieving business objectives. *Making Diversity Work* is unique in the diversity literature in that it provides a structured and realistic approach to achieving an inclusive and diverse workplace. The book treats an often volatile and complex issue in a user-friendly way and is invaluable for both the individual reader and as a resource for management and employee training. This book will be a must for all of our human resource and operations managers at Bausch & Lomb."

—Clayton Osborne, Vice President, Diversity and Organizational Effectiveness, Bausch & Lomb, Inc.

"*Making Diversity Work* is great reading. Not only does Dr. Thiederman provide practical tools for navigating the pathway to diversity, she includes many personal examples that vividly show how biases can pop to the surface and disrupt the productivity of our diverse workplaces. This book is an invaluable tool for anyone determined to make diversity work in their organization."

—Richard Gaskins, Vice President, Diversity, Wyeth Pharmaceuticals

"Am I biased? Yes. Do I need to change my attitude or my behavior? Yes to both. What can I do right now? Work this book, don't just read it. Professionally guided personal work will get us to a healthier place. This book directs that work with realistic case material, diagnostic tools, active solutions, and a deep understanding of human nature. It is part of my personal and professional diversity bag."

—Robert Hayles, Ph.D., Effectiveness/Diversity Consultant, Coauthor of *The Diversity Directive*, 1996 Chair of the Board of Directors, American Society for Training and Development, and Former Vice President, Human Resources and Diversity, The Pillsbury Company

"Dr. Thiederman's new book reminds us that addressing workplace bias is a 'process' of change and not a 'special event' to be undertaken only until something better comes along. From her discussion of the importance of becoming 'mindful of our biases' to how to become 'diversity fit,' she shows us how to negotiate this process most effectively."

—Arthur Jackson, Jr., Vice President, General Administration, Costco Wholesale

"*Making Diversity Work* targets the key reason that many of us resist committing to diversity in the workplace: our own biases. Our workplaces have never been more diverse, and the need for all employees to accept and promote a rainbow work environment is made all the more apparent by the issues raised in this book."

—Michael S. Olson, CAE, Former President and CEO, American Society of Association Executives

"Timely, candid, and practical, *Making Diversity Work* addresses a growing need in today's workplace—how to keep workplace bias from reducing productivity and increasing litigation. The author provides the answer when she challenges us to confront our own biases and develop constructive strategies for overcoming them. We can all benefit by reflecting and acting on the core message of this important new book."

—Stephen O'Connor, Vice President, Government Affairs, Mortgage Bankers Association of America

"Sondra Thiederman's new book will motivate and stimulate employers and employees alike. It removes our bias blinders and allows us to see diversity as a workplace asset. *Making Diversity Work* is a prerequisite for a quality workplace and for life in general."

    —Milton Clipper, President and CEO, Public Broadcasting Atlanta

"*Making Diversity Work* unveils a new paradigm to the world of diversity. Rather than focusing, like most diversity books, on what needs to be done at the organizational level, it argues that we need to take individual responsibility for building effective workplaces. Toward this end, the reader is shown how to challenge personal beliefs and behaviors, how to become aware of biases, and, most important, how to change."

    —Ernest Hicks, Manager, Corporate Diversity, Xerox, Inc.

"Sondra Thiederman has written a fascinating, readable, and hands-on business book that brings the solutions to our diversity challenges to life. Yes, this book is a must-read for every business executive, but it is also an invaluable step-by-step guide for others, including educators, journalists, parents, and (heaven forbid) our political leaders, all of whom must deal with their own and others' often unintentional but still damaging biases. I highly recommend *Making Diversity Work*."

    —David Tulin, President, Tulin DiversiTeam Associates

"Sondra Thiederman gives us an insightful, soul-searching look at how bias takes root in our lives and in the workplace. In each chapter, she offers a new set of lenses with which to see how we can reduce our bias-based behaviors and achieve an improved level of diversity dialogue. This book is a must-read for anyone who is willing to get beyond surface learning about bias and move to 'gut-level' behavioral change!"

    —Edward Hubbard, President, Hubbard & Hubbard, Inc.

"*Making Diversity Work* exposes a harsh reality for many Americans: Nice people have biases and those biases cost us financially, competitively, and personally. This book is an invaluable resource for anyone who is serious about building an inclusive organization."

    —Barbara R. Deane, Editor-in-Chief, DiversityCentral.com and the Cultural Diversity at Work Archive

"With refreshing candor, Dr. Sondra Thiederman has once again contributed a landmark piece of work to the betterment of the field. Through the telling of poignant personal stories about real people, she shows how bias diminishes their ability to achieve full potential. A very practical guide, the book tells us how to address the 'blind spots' that get in the way of fully valuing differences in the workplace."

    —Mary-Frances Winters, President and CEO, The Winters Group, and Author of *Only Wet Babies Like Change* and *Inclusion Starts with "I"*

"At last, a book that talks about bias with the light touch needed to make a delicate subject palatable to all. Sprinkled with humor, *Making Diversity Work* gives us the clear understanding and practical guidelines necessary to learn about our biases, address them, and make the workplace and our lives better for it."

—Julie O'Mara, President, O'Mara and Associates

"Dr. Thiederman captures in her book what so many of us, as managers, are afraid to admit. We become so busy in managing people, meeting deadlines, and staying up with current technology that we rarely stop to analyze how we communicate to the employees we work with daily. Constantly improving our style of communication is key to creating a workplace that is nonthreatening, healthy, and allows people to be appreciated for their individuality. All managers should have a copy of this book in their toolbox."

—Teresa M. Gauger, Acting Deputy Director, Office of Human Resources, Environmental Protection Agency

"I am thoroughly impressed! Sondra Thiederman has found a way to help us all identify the biases we carry. She makes it clear that it is virtually impossible for anyone, even 'nice people,' to be bias free and provides us with a useful mechanism for minimizing their influence on our lives. This innovative volume contains insights that have the power to transform our world and our workplaces."

—Emory Livers, Jr., Director of Diversity, Cincinnati Childrens Hospital Medical Center

"*Making Diversity Work* is a critical contribution to making organizations more productive. Well written, with engaging examples, this book is a great resource for successfully working across all dimensions of difference."

—Judith H. Katz, Ed.D., Executive Vice President, The Kaleel Jamison Consulting Group, Inc., and Author of *The Inclusion Breakthrough: Unleashing the Real Power of Diversity* and *White Awareness: Handbook for Anti-Racism Training*

"Faced with the question, How are you going to deal with all of the differences that you experience in the workplace?, I was happy to learn of Sondra Thiederman's new book, *Making Diversity Work*. This volume is unique among diversity books in that it not only shows us how to take ownership of our own biases, it also provides the reader with valuable strategies for defeating those 'personal fictions' that negatively impact our daily lives."

—Linda Garza Kalaf, MA, SPHR, Manager, Human Resources, America West Airlines

"Stories are the carriers of wisdom and *Making Diversity Work* takes full advantage of this valuable medium of communication. Through page after page of stimulating narrative, the author illustrates how to become aware of our biases and how to suspend them long enough to see the full picture. I recommend this book to you as an instrument for personal advancement and bias reduction. Study it on your own, read it one story at a time in groups, and discuss its implications and lessons. Your thinking will never again shrink to its former limitations."

—Jim Cathcart, Speaker and Author of *Relationship Selling* and *The Acorn Principle*

DEDICATION

For my grandson,
Aiden William Pierce McGinnis.
May you always remember to follow the sound of the bell.

Contents

Foreword   xiii

Acknowledgments   xv

About the Author   xix

Introduction: Truth Be Told   1

PART ONE
THE BASICS OF BIAS

1. *BIAS* DEFINED AND MISDEFINED   19

None of her managers would tell Priscilla that she was doing poorly;
they all wanted to be "nice" to the only black woman in the department.
Were they guilty of bias?

Bias Is an Inflexible Belief about a Particular Kinship Group   19
Case 1: Flexible versus Inflexible—Juan Was Innocent   21
Case 2: "Just Like Me"—I Was Innocent   21
Case 3: "All White People Look Alike"—Ayana Was Innocent   24
Case 4: Reasonable Assumption—Harry Was Innocent   25
Case 5: In the Spirit—Mary Was Innocent   26
Case 6: Guerilla Bias™—Gretchen Was Guilty   26
Ifs, Buts, and Maybes   32

2. CAREFULLY TAUGHT: HOW BIAS IS LEARNED   35

It was her mother's simple admonition not to share her Coke
with the son of the black housekeeper that embedded the seed of bias
deep inside Joan's adolescent psyche.

Immune Deficiency: Why We Contract Biases   36
Initial Infection: Tribal Leaders and Experience   38
The Virus Spreads   41
The Prognosis   43

PART TWO

THE VISION RENEWAL PROCESS

3. STEP ONE: BECOME MINDFUL OF YOUR BIASES 49

When Carrie and her hospital were sued by the Filipino nurse, the manager had no idea what the problem was. Now, too late, Carrie has become aware of her bias against Filipinos and admits she treated them poorly.

Positive ID 50
Strategy I: Observe Your Thoughts 51
Strategy II: Analyze Your Thoughts 54
Strategy III: Measure the Emotional Content of Your Thoughts 56
Strategy IV: Examine Your Attitudes toward Human Difference 57
Conclusion: Looking toward the Next Step 61

4. STEP TWO: IDENTIFY THE ALLEGED BENEFITS OF YOUR BIASES 63

Willy didn't like having a gay man on his team, but his bias convinced him the man was too emotional to handle the stressful job and wouldn't be around for long anyway. For the moment, Willy's bias made him feel more comfortable.

Biases Allegedly Relieve Feelings of Guilt 64
Biases Allegedly Protect Us from Diminished Status 65
Biases Allegedly Protect Us from Loss 66
Biases Allegedly Protect Us from Emotional Pain 67
Biases Allegedly Provide Us with an Excuse for Our Behavior 68
Biases Allegedly Protect Our Community and Individual Values 70
Conclusion: A Cautionary Note 71

5. STEP THREE: PUT YOUR BIASES THROUGH TRIAGE 73

When Linda's bias caused her to lose a top sales associate to her main competition, she lost, along with a valuable employee, thousands of dollars in convention business.

Does Your Bias Compromise Your Ability to Hire the Best People? 74
Does Your Bias Interfere with Your Ability to Retain Quality Employees? 76
Does Your Bias Interfere with Corporate Productivity and Individual Success? 79
Does Your Bias Interfere with Your Ability to Sustain Harmonious Teams? 80
Does Your Bias Compromise the Success of Your Sales Efforts? 81
Does Your Bias Put Your Organization at Risk for Litigation? 84
Conclusion: Preparing for the Next Step 85

6. STEP FOUR: DISSECT YOUR BIASES 87

Hannah, a top executive, just couldn't get rid of her bias that "All men are sexist." That is until she realized that her belief grew out of only three bad experiences in her long career. Once she figured that out, she was able to see men as individuals, not as reflections of her painful past.

The Inquisition 88
Glad to Make Your Acquaintance 92

7. STEP FIVE: IDENTIFY COMMON KINSHIP GROUPS 95

Tom who is white and Mai who is Asian didn't realize how much they had in common until discovering that they both knew what it was like to feel out of place because of the color of their skin.

How Sharing a Kinship Group Reduces Bias 96
Acknowledge a Shared "Race" 98
Acknowledge Shared Emotion 100
Look for a Shared Work Ethic 109
Create a Shared Goal 110
Identify a Shared Humanity 112

8. STEP SIX: SHOVE YOUR BIASES ASIDE 115

Jill almost didn't hire Lance because he was over 50 and she figured he couldn't do the job. Luckily, she shoved her bias that older people are uncreative aside and hired one of the most innovative professionals her department had ever seen.

9. STEP SEVEN: BEWARE THE BIAS REVIVAL 119

No matter how hard she tried, Bess's bias that people with accents are less intelligent kept popping back up. Finally, she decided to treat everyone as if they knew what they were doing. The result? Improved performance and a bias that once again went into remission.

The Reluctant Patient 120
Individual Encounters and Resuscitating Events 121
Fake It Till You Make It 123
Pass the Buck 126

PART THREE
GATEWAY EVENTS:
Entering into Diversity Dialogue

10. THE BENEFITS OF DIVERSITY DIALOGUE 133

When Jane heard what her boss said about her, she was ready to sue for discrimination. Fortunately, she mentioned the rumor

to him before taking action and discovered that he had been
badly misunderstood.

Benefit: Increased Knowledge and Understanding   134
Benefit: Rumor Reduction   136
Benefit: The Stifled Spread of Bias   138

11. GETTING DIVERSITY FIT   141

When the man in the wheelchair accused her of bias against him,
the woman froze. What could she do? She knew he was wrong,
but was too diversity unfit to know how to respond.

Conclusion: Preparing for the Next Step   144

12. COGNITIVE SKILLS FOR DIVERSITY DIALOGUE   147

Despite the fact that the speaker was a strong supporter of diversity,
when his talk was over, a woman raised her hand and accused him of
bias because he used the word "guys." What would you have done?

Resist, Remember, Rethink   148
Identify Your Goals   152
Recognize a Common Enemy   158
Recognize Mutual Contributions   159
Build on the Pyramid Principle   163

13. VERBAL SKILLS FOR DIVERSITY DIALOGUE   165

Charmaine was ready to sue. She was certain she had lost the
promotion because she was gay. She was certain, that is, until her boss
showed his respect for her by really listening to what she had to say.

Employ Verbal and Vocal Modulation   166
Avoid Dogmatic Language   168
Maintain a High Standard   170
Strive for Creative Communication   170
Really Listen   171
Conclusion: Living Anywhere We Want   173

Conclusion: Moment of Truth   175
Appendix: Reader's Guide   179
Endnotes   191
Index   195

▐ have read many books and papers
on diversity and have been part of many discussions on the subject as the
CEO of a company that has been at the leading edge of the subject.
However, *Making Diversity Work: Seven Steps for Defeating Bias in the Workplace* truly advances the art of making diversity work.

Its title suggests that it is targeted to the workplace, but the insights
offered go far beyond workplace diversity. Its starting point is that it is
most important to understand others as complete individuals, not solely
by reference to race, gender, national origin, ethnicity, sexual orientation, or disability. These attributes are essential to our understanding
but should not limit how we look at others. Ultimately, every human
being has a set of experiences and values that defines them, and if we
are to be effective at interpersonal relations, we need to understand
them better through conversation. By framing the problem the way she
has, Dr. Thiederman makes it clear that every individual has the problem of biased attitudes, and that each of us can take steps to reduce bias.

Dr. Thiederman acknowledges that this task is uncomfortable, because it denies us the apparent safe haven of categorizing people permanently by one or more defining characteristics. She recognizes that
we need some hooks on which to hang assessment of people from time
to time, but also points out the dangers of staying with a static assessment.
She points out that individuals are more complex and unique than any
categorization can indicate, and that they evolve over time as well.

Dr. Thiederman also challenges the notion that we are being "nice"
to others by denying them an in-depth assessment as unique individuals
and by not sharing that assessment in candid but respectful feedback.
She makes the commonsense, but often ignored, observation that we evidence more care and concern by telling others what they *need* to hear,
rather than by treating them as if they were fragile works of art.

We also can gain great insight from the frank way in which she
points out that diversity works only if those who have been the subject of

discrimination treat others with the same fairness and individuality as they should appropriately demand.

Dr. Thiederman is practical in giving the reader tools to move from a biased orientation to one that is as free from bias as human beings can achieve. Finally, she is helpful in recognizing that there are many opportunities in day-to-day interpersonal relationships for us to move from bias to a more individualized understanding of others, and that those "gateway" opportunities, as she characterizes them, while not easy to recognize or prepare for, need to be seized.

Her perspective is unique, very valuable, but very challenging. The best books I read take my thinking to a different level of knowledge and insight. This is one I highly recommend for those who want that kind of experience.

—Michael I. Critelli, Chairman and CEO of Pitney Bowes, Inc.

Four days and five nights in an isolated cabin in the San Jacinto mountains and the book is almost finished; just a polish or two here and there remains to be done, but I guess that tweaking can go on forever. It is odd to think that I am finally near the end. It has been four plus years of stops and starts and rethinkings, all of which would have come to nothing if not for the input and support of many individuals along the way.

Most authors traditionally place the most important people at the end of the Acknowledgments, sort of like an Oscar acceptance speech in which the high school drama teacher comes first followed by parents, spouse, and, finally, a deity. I realize most folks don't read Acknowledgments through to the finish and because I wouldn't want any mistake about the identity of my most important support person, I decided to break with tradition and mention him first: my husband, Tom Sandler. You will meet him and his diversity foibles from time to time throughout the book. He may, as you will discover, not be a perfect man when it comes to bias, but then again, who is? In most other ways, however, Tom is pretty amazing. It was Tom who encouraged me when I felt this book would never come to fruition, who took care of the bits and pieces of living in these final weeks so that I would have the psychological room in which to complete the task, and who sent me off to this cabin fully stocked with supplies and fueled with his good wishes, love, and support. For these things, and myriad others, I will always be grateful.

There would be no book, of course, if not for those folks who were generous and brave enough to share with me their embarrassments, successes, and even their bias disasters. That kind of openness is a lot to ask, especially in today's climate where "guilty till proven innocent" of bias is the order of the day. The initial batch of brave souls who came forward were encountered informally in the few moments following dozens of workshops and speeches on diversity that I have presented throughout the years. These contributions amounted to little more than snippets of thought and experience voiced casually at the front of the room or over cups of coffee and stale pastry. Despite their brevity these tiny tales gradually seeped into my consciousness and formed a shape that suddenly looked suspiciously like a more enlightened way to confront the challenge of bias and optimistically like a book that had to be written.

Other contributors were formally interviewed. The identities of some of these people, through their choice or mine, are hidden behind pseudonyms or composite characters; each of you know who you are and I thank you for what you added to this project. Others have participated more openly. In no particular order, these include: Barbara Ceconi, Kurt Kuss, Steve Hanamura, Tony Polk, Elena Panduro, Krista Sandler, Deborah Helm, Åke Sandler, Gayle Brock, Amber Caffall, Prue Drummond, Shea and Josh McGinnis, Singer Buchanan, Susan Swan, Martha Mason, Booker Izell, Kevin Moore, Duane Roth, Joan and Bob Pierce, Paco Sevilla, Shelley Schwarz, Cathy Rudd, Nancy and Bill Bamburger, Stephanie Britton, Jessica Moore, Jim Lonergan, Julie Madigan, Alexander Hicks, Cherly DeLeon, Amy and Mark Jackson, Robert Marks, Sr., Jim Adamson, and Roger Ackerman. In addition, I must extend a very special thanks to Zhao Lin Chen whose elegantly simple story of his new life in America reminded me why this country is so great and why we must continue our efforts to resolve the conflicts that have so long divided us. I am grateful, too, to Deborah Pourali whose enthusiasm early on in the project helped acquire much fascinating material, including the story of Mr. Chen, scientist turned crossing guard.

There are others who did not contribute stories per se, but whose existence refined my thinking and helped bring this narrative to life. Among these are the mysterious Harvard graduate in Chapter 10; Louis, who taught me an important lesson about how mistaken we can sometimes be about the identity of our own biases; Manny Davis, the finest limousine driver on the eastern seaboard; the anonymous and possibly angry young man in that Westwood, California, gas station; and, finally, "Candace," who reminded me in some ways of my childhood friend Karen Johnson. By the way, in anticipation of writing this book, I tried and failed to locate Karen. Karen, if you see this, call me! I'll take you to dinner and in honor of Candace this time we'll do it right.

Because so much of the philosophy of this book is rooted in current workplace events and individual experiences, previously published material played a secondary importance in my thinking. That is, with one exception: Bruce Jacobs's marvelous book *Race Manners*. When I plucked Bruce's small black-and-white volume off the shelf of the local Barnes & Noble, I had no idea what it was. I did know, however, that it was reasonably priced and easy to carry so I decided to buy it. After several weeks of plowing through less fruitful sources, I finally found a moment to look at *Race Manners* and in that moment I discovered an uncommon blend of painful truth, practical solutions, and pure poetry. Thank you, Bruce, for writing a book that inspired me and informed my efforts in ways I could never have anticipated.

The list of those who helped with this project continues to expand—from those who performed consultation and editorial duties to the friends and colleagues who were kind enough to read the manuscript with an eye toward making sure I hadn't gone off the deep end. These include: Julie O'Mara, Claire Ginther, Alan Richter, Roosevelt Thomas, Price Cobbs, Anne Rippey, Åke Sandler, Joann Nowka, Shea McGinnis, Gloria Applegate, Barbara Deane, Michael Wheeler, and Gretchen Van Maren.

My thanks to agent Andrea Pedolsky who led me to Dearborn Trade. Once there, it became a pleasure working with Jon Malysiak and the staff. Their expertise and experience have relieved the strain that so often accompanies journeys through the confusing world of publishing.

And then there is Joan Pierce, my friend and assistant who has been my sidekick and unflagging support for almost a decade. I am grateful to Joan for so many things, including her holding down the fort when I complained of not enough uninterrupted time; her tolerating my short-term memory failure over details that I know made her job, particularly in recent months, a great deal harder; and, of course, her insightful read of the initial and subsequent manuscripts. Mostly, however, I want to thank Joan for her tireless enthusiasm for and confidence in the virtue of this project. Writing a book in isolation is tough, and even though Joan now works from a very remote location, her encouragement is so powerful it feels as if it is spilling, as it used to, out of her old office just six feet down the hall.

Although they are not here to see this publication, I also want to thank the pair of "ambivalent racists" referred to in Chapter 2: my mother and father. You will learn a lot about my parents in these pages, but one thing that will not emerge is how they instilled in me the virtue of hard work. This was a lesson learned, not so much through discipline or elaborate reward, but through support and quiet encouragement. The support I remember best came from my mother, who, during those long study nights of my high school years, had a way of magically appearing from the kitchen bearing nourishment at the exact moment it was needed. That moment usually fell around two o'clock in the morning and the nourishment came in the form of a bowl of sliced bananas and cream with just a little sugar sprinkled on top. Never once did she admonish me to go to bed or say I needed my rest; all she did was bring the bananas and the cream—that was all the encouragement I needed.

Finally, I want to acknowledge the person to whom this book is dedicated, my grandson Aiden. With his crooked two-year old grin and independent spirit, Aiden William Pierce McGinnis charms everyone who crosses his rambunctious path. I have no doubt that his mother and I are only the first in a long line of women who will be inexorably, permanently, and unapologetically biased in this young man's favor.

Sondra Thiederman, Ph.D., is one of the nation's leading experts on bias reduction, workplace diversity, and cross-cultural business. Based in San Diego, she is a sought-after speaker who brings 25 years' experience to presentations that motivate and entertain while providing practical results to organizations as diverse as General Motors, UBS PaineWeber, Marriott Corporation, Pfizer Pharmaceuticals, American Express, Xerox, and AT&T.

She is the recipient of a doctorate in cross-cultural studies from UCLA, is the author of two previous books, and has served as a consultant to the University of California. Appointed to the American Red Cross Diversity Cabinet by Elizabeth Dole, Dr. Thiederman has been widely featured in the media, including in the *New York Times, Nation's Business, Entrepreneur,* the *Los Angeles Times,* and *U.S. News & World Report.*

In her continuing efforts to better understand how diverse people can work together more effectively, she welcomes your insights and experiences. Kindly direct your comments as well as any inquiries for speaking or training to: e-mail: STPhD@Thiederman.com; Web site: <www.Thiederman.com>; or phone: 800-858-4478.

$T r u t h$ **B** e **T** $o l d$

Karen Johnson and I were best friends in junior high school. She was one of only three black kids in our neighborhood and, although I would never admit it, one reason I was her friend was that she was black and I was white and that made me just a little bit of a rebel and I liked that. OK, I admit it, lie number one. When the time came to move on to high school, Karen and I drifted apart. We pretended it was just because of the natural ebb and flow of friendship at a formative age and never mentioned it, but one of the reasons we were no longer friends was because of her blackness and my whiteness. There it is: lie number two.

And on and on they go, lies and fibs and, at the very least, naive statements we tell ourselves and each other about how we feel about people who are different from ourselves. Perhaps we pretend that we never notice the color of a person's skin; maybe we, as organizations, deny the reality that bias can be hidden behind well-meaning efforts to accommodate diverse employees; other times, we honor false accusations of bias while ignoring the real discrimination that is harder to identify and tougher to resolve. No matter what form the dishonesty takes, it is lies like these that are largely responsible for the glacially slow progress corporations are making in removing bias from the workplace.

LUCRATIVE VIRTUE

This sluggish pace is unfortunate because bias—that tendency to prejudge others according to the group to which they belong—costs American business and Americans themselves dearly in lost opportunities, ruined relationships, and broken hearts. More tangibly, bias is sapping American business of time, energy, and, in the end, money. Executives and managers squander time and money warding off discrimination suits and excessive turnover; employees waste precious energy on the tensions and misunderstandings found in their diverse workplaces; and sales associates sacrifice lucrative deals because bias cripples their ability to accurately interpret customer needs. Each one of these problems is the direct result of allowing bias to distort our view of who people really are—to create, in essence, case after case of mistaken identity. These figures will give you a rough idea of what is at stake.

The price of bias: Litigation. Discrimination suits are every executive's nightmare. This is, of course, no surprise when you look at figures like the $192 million, $157 million, and $176 million paid out by Coca-Cola, State Farm Insurance, and Texaco, respectively. Admittedly, most companies do not face damages as large as these, but even the more modest amounts ($3.5 million paid by Footlocker Specialty and $14.4 million by Northwest Airlines) combined with the hidden expense of attorneys' fees, Employment Practices Liability (EPL) insurance, court costs, out-of-court settlements, and loss of reputation are enough to take the gloss off of anyone's annual report.

The price of bias: Lost employees. Both the hidden and direct costs of losing good employees are shockingly high. These can range from 25 percent of an annual salary up to 250 percent and beyond.[1] These figures become still more disconcerting when we consider the specific loss of minority professionals whose recruitment costs include referral bonuses to colleagues, money spent on executive search teams, and, of course, the loss of the creativity and innovation that is characteristic of most diverse work teams.

The price of bias: Diminished sales and lost customers. A look at the following facts proves that sales associates and customer service professionals cannot afford to let bias interfere with their ability to relate appropriately to diverse customers:

- The combined spending of blacks, Asian-Americans, and Native Americans will be $1.4 trillion by the year 2007.
- By that same year, Latinos in the United States will have a buying power of approximately $1 billion.[2]
- Gay and lesbian consumers have substantially more discretionary income than do heterosexuals.[3]

If these figures aren't enough to convince you that we must get our biases under control, consider the fact that team members who work increasingly in an international environment must be able to accurately assess the needs of colleagues and customers of all cultures.

The price of bias: Wasted time. Managers throw away dozens of hours each year mediating bias-related conflicts. This wasted time is a tangible and measurable drain on company resources. Diversity consultant Edward Hubbard has developed a straightforward way to calculate the cost: Multiply the manager's hourly rate by the number of hours spent on nonmission critical work. By performing this simple calculation, we see immediately why companies can ill afford to waste expensive time on problems created by bias.[4]

The ability to overcome bias is obviously a lucrative virtue and a skill we all need to acquire if we are to convert workplace tension into a powerful force of productivity, progress, and profits.

WHO WILL BENEFIT FROM THIS BOOK?

This book might have been titled, *The Nice Person's Guide to Bias Reduction.* It is not about blatant discrimination, interracial hatred, or violent homophobia. These ailments are relatively simple to deal with mostly because they and their perpetrators are easy to spot. They bring with them no gray areas, no subtleties of motivation, and few decisions to be made about the cure: Ask the offender to leave. *Making Diversity Work* is concerned instead with the subtler forms of bias—the ones held by otherwise nice people (that's you and me and most of the folks we know) and that are insidious in the harm they do to our workplaces, our communities, and ourselves. Just because we are nice people, however, does not let us off the hook. Maybe none of us would dream of firing someone because of his or her religion or for telling an antigay joke, but to mangle Samuel Johnson with a paraphrase of my own:

> The tribe is numerous of those who lull their own responsibility with the remembrance of biases more destructive than their own. We must judge our individual virtue, not against the measure of those who fail, but against the elevated standard of those who succeed.

We need to maintain Johnson's elevated standard regardless of what type of diversity we work with and what particular strain of bias plagues us. This book will help you achieve this goal whether your issues pertain to ethnicity, disabilities, personal appearance, religion, gender, what we commonly refer to as race, age, sexual orientation, or any other type of human difference. In particular, *Making Diversity Work* will be helpful to you if you are:

- *An executive* who is responsible for maintaining a competitive advantage, increasing productivity within a diverse workforce, and staving off costly discrimination suits.
- *A manager* who wastes valuable time mediating bias and discrimination-induced conflicts.
- *A human resources professional* who is charged with recruiting and retaining qualified diverse employees and whose responsibilities include coaching and conflict mediation.
- *A supervisor* who is responsible for accurately interpreting the needs and motivation style of a diverse work team.
- *A diversity director* who requires a fresh and practical tool for creating workplace harmony, increasing productivity, and educating people about how to make diversity work.
- *A sales associate* who needs to increase revenue among prospects of diverse backgrounds.
- *A customer service representative* who must see all people accurately to appropriately meet their needs and expectations.
- *An international business professional* who interacts with colleagues and customers from a variety of cultures.
- *A human being* who needs to see people more accurately, build better relationships, and become more professionally successful.

"BUT EVERYBODY DOES IT"

Even as you read this, you may be thinking that you are one of the innocent ones—one of the good guys who sees past skin color and accent and lifestyle to the person beneath. You may have been driven to pick up this book because you are a target of bias, but certainly, or so you think, not because you are a perpetrator. Admittedly, you probably are more innocent than the man who commits a hate crime or the woman who uses a racial slur, but I wager that you have your own share of biases—what I call personal fictions—and, like the rest of us, have something to learn about seeing people more accurately.

No one is blameless when it comes to bias. Sure, some biases are launched from a more rarified height by the most powerful and hit their target with greater force, but, ultimately, bias is bias. No one group's bigotry has any more or less cache than another's. Because of this panhuman guilt, I have applied myself not one bit more to the task of helping men honor women than women honor men; helping Christians respect Muslims than Muslims respect Christians; or helping whites respect blacks than blacks respect whites. This book is as concerned with reducing the biases of a person with a disability as those of the fully abled, as directed to heterophobes as at homophobes. No one group is more a beneficiary or more a target than another.

In that connection, *Making Diversity Work* is filled with all kinds of biases and all complexions of villains. White villains, black villains, gay villains, and—what a shocker—even a disabled villain or two. Susan, an employee at the Equal Employment Opportunity Commission, of all places, is one of these offenders. Here's what she says about some of her most disliked clients:

> I don't want to put one group down, but when I listen to EEOC complaints, it always seems that it is the black people who are most angry and unreasonable. It makes my job very difficult and sometimes I just stop caring.

White racist, you say? Terrible thing that she is employed at this particular job? Well, the news is that Susan is black and she is also frustrated and overloaded, and, as we'll see later in this book, she may not be such a villain after all.

If you still need convincing that the only bias we need to fight is in the hearts of the so-called Anglo-Saxon majority, read what happened as I drove from the airport with the Jewish owner of a small limousine service. The driver was all too willing to dump his biased views on a total stranger:

> I had barely stowed my luggage when the man began complaining about his difficulties in getting reliable employees. He said proudly that he would hire anyone—blacks, Spanish, Greeks—anyone except, as he put it, "ragheads." Claiming that "they are all bums," he admitted, with little awareness of how this same scenario might have played out against his own immigrant parents, that "When they call and I hear the accent, I tell them the job is filled. As far as I'm concerned, those ragheads ought to go back from where they came." When I asked him how he knew that they "all" are so bad, this otherwise apparently

intelligent man responded with a very definite, "I hired one once and he was no good. Once burned, I've learned my lesson."

I thought of this man on September 11, 2001, and hoped against hope that no ragheads ever again tried to approach him when they needed a job.

Another myth about who has biases pertains to men and women. Somewhere along the line, we got the idea that the only sexism that exists flows from the intolerant hearts of men. Well, take a look inside this shuttle bus as it loaded up the first morning of a women's technology conference and you'll see how wrong this assumption is. Things were fine as long as there were only women on the bus, then, suddenly, everything changed:

> As the conference attendees gradually boarded the shuttle, each new female passenger was greeted with enthusiasm. Each was asked where she was from and what brought her to the conference, and was offered other verbal niceties designed to make her feel welcome. Also, more often than not, someone would move her briefcase and invite the newcomer to sit down. Then, as if he were an apparition from Mars, a man mounted the steps. He was about 40 years old, white, five foot, ten inches tall, pleasant looking, and, judging from his deliberate stare straight down the center aisle, more than a little uncomfortable. Why? Because not one woman greeted him. No cheerful hellos, no words of welcome, no polite inquiries were issued to relieve his discomfort, and, most telling of all, not one woman offered him a seat beside her.

Had this situation been reversed, had the bus been filled with men and the new arrival been a woman, there would have been irate outcries of bias, discrimination, exclusion, and worse: sexism. Incidents like this are irrefutable evidence that intergender bias is a two-way street.

Susan and the limousine driver and many of the women on that bus no doubt have had plenty of experience being targets of bigotry. You would think that they would learn from that pain and be determined not to inflict it on others. Sadly, cases like these and dozens of others throughout the book show us that human thought processes are often not logical and, as one contributor put it, "Suffering does not always bring enlightenment."

BIAS BUSTING: IT CAN BE DONE

In view of how much biases cost us and the fact that they are found in all segments of the population, it is good news that we can do something about them. We are, after all, not born biased. There is no genetic predisposition to bias, no bias gene rides on our chromosomes, there is no DNA test that can identify who is biased and who is not. Bias is learned. It is an acquired habit of thought rooted in fear and fueled by conditioning and, as such, can be unacquired and deconditioned. Of course, some biases are so deeply imbedded in the mosaic of culture that it would take a jackhammer to dislodge them. The Nazi belief that Jews are inferior or the skinhead doctrine of white superiority fall into this category. Beliefs such as these take on more than just the status of bias; they are also cultural values and norms. It is not that the steps in this book can't be useful in weakening such norms, but, heinous though they are, they are not our primary target. *Making Diversity Work* is designed, instead, to erode the tragically numerous garden-variety biases held by you and me—the nice people of the world.

You nice people will find the heart of the healing process in Part Two, "The Vision Renewal Process" (VRP). I chose this name because what bias does is interfere with our ability to see people accurately, hence the need to renew our vision. The VRP consists of seven steps. It begins with strategies for becoming aware of our biases and moves systematically toward learning to shove our biases aside and, finally, immunize ourselves from the relapse that so often accompanies personal growth.

The Vision Renewal Process and the principles on which it is based were developed through years of research and contact with contributors met during two decades of speaking and training on diversity and bias issues. The spark for the book's point of view, however, came from personal experience and from my own efforts to understand the biases within myself. You will catch glimpses of those efforts throughout this volume. From my youthful friendship with Karen Johnson to a conversation about clothes and men with a woman who closely resembled a grown-up Karen on a bar stool in a San Diego restaurant, it has been a complex journey and one that has no end.

Part Three, "Gateway Events: Entering into Diversity Dialogue," continues the attack on bias, but does so from a different flank. This section provides the tools necessary to carry on productive dialogue in the face of those awkward and sometimes frightening encounters that can happen when we work with people who are different from ourselves. The reason these tools will further reduce bias is that conversation—especially conversation in response to conflict—increases understanding and increased understanding is what bias reduction is all about.

TERMS OF ART

Without a shared language, however, all the effort in the world to rid ourselves of bias will be wasted. We need to clarify what lawyers call our shared *terms of art*. Terms of art are words and phrases that communicate very specific ideas. The world of law requires this precision, but so, too, does the world of diversity. Sadly, that precision is dangerously lacking. The term *sexism*, for example, has come to apply to offenses as broad-ranging as commenting on a female colleague's appearance to banning women from the boardroom. *Racism* no longer means just gross acts of exclusion and cruelty, but also events as innocent as misidentifying a person's race or being ignorant of the latest group labels. Because words like *racism, sexism, stereotype, homophobia,* and *prejudice* have become so vague and exaggerated, I have chosen to minimize their use and employ instead the term *bias* to encompass the essence of them all. For the sake of variety, I will from time to time use *prejudice, stereotype, misbelief,* or *personal fiction* as substitutes for *bias*. In every case, regardless of the term, bias results in cases of mistaken identity in which we are unable to see others accurately. We will look in Chapter 1 at what does and does not lie within the parameters of these terms, but for now this definition will get us started:

> *A bias is an inflexible positive or negative prejudgment about the nature, character, and abilities of an individual and is based on a generalized idea about the group to which the person belongs.*

Another area of confusion over the lexicon of diversity has to do with the sticky issue of what to call members of particular groups. Is it Latino or Hispanic?, black or African-American?, Asian or Oriental? Is ladies acceptable or does that imply a confinement to Victorian roles and prudish social restrictions? Are white people white, Anglo, or Caucasian, or do we make a real project out of it and call them Euro-Americans? It really becomes fun when we try to focus on that wavy dateline that separates Generation X from their younger siblings, the Net Generation, and the Net Generation from their juniors, the Millennium Generation. I, for example, grew up convinced I was a baby boomer and was vaguely proud of it. Much to my chagrin, I recently discovered that a 1944 birth date—even one as late as September—disqualified me from boomer status and left me languishing with my older colleagues in the Traditionalist generation.

Keeping terminology straight may be a chore, but it does matter. Admittedly, our culture has carried all this too far—changing *manhole* to *personhole* and classic quotes from history to conform to the he/she doctrine is ridiculous—but at times respect for groups mandates the careful choice of terms. Terms are symbolic of proud origins, of position in society, and of who brokers power and who does not. The problem is that not everyone of one group wants to be called the same thing. I learned this following a workshop in which I variously used Latino and Hispanic, black and African-American. During the break, four people protested my use of these terms: One didn't like Latino, one complained about Hispanic, one derided my use of black, and the fourth said he was offended by African-American. Right then and there I decided to continue to make a reasonable effort to keep up with current preferences but, having done that, ultimately use the terms with which I am most comfortable. Hence my choices in this book of black, not African-American, Latino as opposed to Hispanic, and white rather then Anglo.

One word I really dislike is that most archaic of jargon, *minority*. If there was ever a term whose time has passed, this is it. Even the city council of San Diego, California, a relatively conservative community, voted to have the term banned from use in city documents, stricken from past documents, and exchanged for *people of color*. I am no fan of people of color, it is limited in scope and awkward, but at least it doesn't carry the pejorative and antiquated tone of minority. To refer to someone as a minority is like calling the American West wild, Russia a superpower, or China a third world country. The term is particularly ridiculous in my home state of California where no group is a majority. How can there be a minority when there no longer is a majority? Activists have substituted the term *oppressed* for *minority* with the tragic result that these groups are now firmly positioned in the national psyche as powerless victims. I have even seen *diverse people* used—another example of linguistic nonsense since everyone on the planet is diverse in the sense of being different from someone else.

For these reasons, I have chosen to call those who have previously been labeled minority or oppressed or diverse as *emerging groups*. Emerging group shifts the emphasis from past wrongs to current solutions and future equality. Also, it serves the positive function of repositioning the oppressed or minority in our culture from a population that is lacking in position to a group that is moving forward to greater achievement and empowerment. It is also a term that, if we work hard to reduce bias in our country, will eventually sound as obsolete as *Oriental* and *colored* do today. These groups will have emerged.

Another term that I have coined is *kinship group*. A kinship group is any population that shares a self-ascribed or externally ascribed characteristic that sets it apart from others. This characteristic might be a shared occupation, sexual orientation, personal interest, physical ability, gender, race, ethnicity, thinking style, or any other unifying factor. Because it can apply to any characteristic, the term *kinship group* emphasizes and respects the complexities of what people share and how they differ. One of the advantages of the phrase is that it allows each individual to be identified and valued in an unlimited number of human dimensions. It enables, for example, an Asian engineer who is also a mother responsible for her elderly parents to connect to other Asians, but also to women of all ethnic backgrounds, male engineers, and anyone who is responsible for dependents of all ages. In this sense, kinship group allows for group pride but does so without implying a state of victimhood; the phrase also encourages people to look for what they share. Another advantage to this phrase is that it excludes no one; even white males form a kinship group and as such are included as much in the discussion of diversity as any other population.

Finally, you will notice that I tend to use the word *target* instead of *victim* for those individuals or groups that have biases directed against them. This choice is dictated by the philosophical thrust of the book that we each have a responsibility to resist being oppressed by the biases around us. As we will see in these pages, we are all targets of one kind of bias or another; we become victims only when we allow that bias to defeat us in some way.

WHAT THIS BOOK IS NOT

One thing *Making Diversity Work* is not is a consistently pleasant read. At times you will feel uncomfortable. Some of the points made will be hard to take, some of the truths will be hard to look at. On top of that, underlying every word is the message that every one of us is obligated to make an effort to overcome bias in ourselves and in those around us. There is no passing the buck to the other guy, to the men, to the majority, or to the tragedies of history. Bias lies in every heart and every mind—it is there also that the answers lie. The light is at your end of the tunnel and it is up to you to carry that light to the other side. No one has a corner on bias and no one is spared the obligation to eradicate it.

This book is also not an encyclopedia. The anecdotes and examples used do not reflect a desire nor an effort to cover the concerns of all kinship groups equally nor is it balanced in terms of addressing all the ways in which bias can negatively impact our lives. The material that I chose to include was driven by two things. First, by the desire to correct specific distortions in our thinking about bias, and second, by the nature of the stories and interviews that my associates and I gathered. Someone once said, "Anecdotes multiplied become data." I am not pretending that the anecdotes contained in this book amount to any kind of data. Instead they are devices chosen to illustrate and animate the key points of each chapter.

With respect to the kind of material found here, you will notice that both anecdotes and commentary are weighted in the direction of black and white racial issues. This was not my intention; I simply received more anecdotes about relationships between blacks and whites than about gender differences, disabilities, or sexual orientation. This heavy emphasis on racial differences is less distorting to the solutions presented here than you might think. Black and white racism is, after all, the defining bias of our nation; it is the archetype of all isms and, as such, provides lessons that apply to all other biases. If you can handle racial bias, you can handle anything.

Making Diversity Work is also not a compendium of absolute answers. There are never concrete, 100-percent-applicable solutions when it comes to human beings and bias, for bias is a uniquely human foible. Like the human mind, the terrain of diversity is more like an undulating ocean with an ever-changing seascape than a piece of easily navigated farmland. Vantage points are ever shifting, sea-lanes come and go. Part of the function of this book is to provide devices to help you navigate that ocean and begin to feel comfortable with the changes it perpetually serves up.

For those of you seeking legal prescriptions for what is and is not acceptable in the workplace, *Making Diversity Work* is not for you. You won't learn what words can be safely uttered nor what behaviors are actionable; you will learn, however, something far more valuable:

You will learn to diminish in yourself and others the fundamental attitudes that generate inappropriate behavior.

Although we may never be able to create a perfect world nor a perfect workplace, the goal of this book is to reduce bias to the point where we no longer need to be thoroughly schooled in political correctness or even specific rules of the law. Because our attitude toward differences will be informed and enlightened, we will be able to behave automatically and unself-consciously in ways that are appropriate, legal, and effective.

This book is also not about redressing the sins of the past, it is about starting now and moving forward. We can no longer let past pain weaken emerging groups and distract them from achieving excellence. Nor can the descendants of oppressors allow their genetic sins to weaken their resolve to do the right thing from this moment forward. We have a lot of good reasons and excuses to jump into the past, but the answers lie in the present and future. That is good news because it means we have power. Knowledge of the past is the foundation for action, but forward is the only direction open to us.

Finally, as upsetting as this might be to my professors at the University of California at Los Angeles, this volume is not intended to be objective nor scholarly in the sense of recounting a compendium of facts that are universally agreed upon. *Making Diversity Work* has a point of view and a message to sell and that message is clear: We all need to tell the truth about bias and use that truth to do the moral thing and work to overcome the enemy. Yes, I said that unpopular word *moral*. I believe in right and wrong. There is no situational morality when it comes to bias; it is wrong under any circumstance, anywhere, anytime, no matter who the perpetrator and no matter who the target.

THE CHALLENGE AND THE LEARNING

I come from a storytelling family. As far back as I can remember, we practically catalogued incidents that amused, stroked our egos, contained a lesson, or simply made life more fun. I remember my father telling of a solar eclipse on a winter day in the New Jersey countryside. He spoke eloquently of the ice crunching under his feet and the trees casting distorted shadows in the snow. I also recall my mother's recollections of her nursing days and the time she received a champion Airedale and a diamond watch from a grateful patient. Then there was the one about the Union Pacific Railway and my father's trek across the country to become part of the golden age of Hollywood in the 1940s. It is because of this penchant for storytelling that I decided to let the focus of this book follow the stories contributed by those who have had experience with bias.

When my staff and I first set out to gather this material, we anticipated an easy task. After all, we figured, people are always coming to me

after presentations to tell of their latest diversity encounter; why would it be any different under these circumstances? We could not have been more wrong. Gathering personal experiences became a real challenge. When asked a question like "Can you share with me an incident in which you learned something about how to overcome a bias?" even those who were involved with diversity and worked with bias issues daily came up blank. We heard "Sorry, I can't think of anything" so often and from so many different types of people that we knew there had to be more to this blankness than just lack of experiences. When we explored more deeply, we came to two conclusions. First, some of the potential contributors, despite their numerous experiences involving bias, were simply unaware of how the dynamics worked, what they felt about what happened, or what their problems were.

Although this was discouraging in terms of having enough material, it made us realize how much this book was needed. The second conclusion we reached was that people are afraid to confront the issue of bias, even, or especially, within themselves. Quite frankly, I don't blame them. To look honestly at a conflict or even a relatively benign interaction involving bias can be frightening and even painful, mostly because every such exploration involves the risk of learning something unpleasant about ourselves. One thing I hope this book will do is provide the tools to make examining our biases less threatening and, therefore, more productive.

Once we adjusted our interview strategies to compensate for these barriers, the stories began to flood in. At that point, however, we encountered another problem: More often than not, what we received were tales of sexism, discrimination, hurt feelings, and offense. Although I am sure that the teller of each story felt the pain reflected in the account, I doubt that the sheer number of victim stories provided an accurate perspective on the state of bias in the American workplace. We soon realized that although most of these stories were true, their sheer numbers were exaggerated by the fact that people who feel victimized are compelled to talk about it. Less interesting, and less on our minds, are those incidents in which two people found an unexpected bond, solved an interpersonal problem with aplomb, or overcame a bias by working together. The negative compels us to talk to find relief; the positive just rests comfortably in our memory. Discouraging as these results were, they opened up an entirely new avenue of thinking about the dynamics of victimhood, the power of perception, and the importance of shifting the discussion from complaints about the problem to suggestions for solutions.

WHITE MISCHIEF

The biggest challenge in writing this book was getting myself out of the way of the process. I failed. Every story, every idea is filtered through my values and my perspective. For one thing, I alone chose, combined, and edited the stories to be included. Every incident is based on what really happened in the workplace, but I have to admit that certain situations sparked my interest, others reinforced my point of view, and some were couched in language that appealed to my aesthetic sensibilities. In some cases, I played psychic and even guessed at what the characters were thinking—a practice that I strongly discourage in real life. No matter what the choice, each one was dictated by my own cultures and upbringing.

The most pertinent of those cultures, particularly in view of the subject of this book, is the way of thinking that comes with my white middle-class background. Anyone who knows me knows I am a stereotype of whiteness. I was raised in the 1950s and 1960s in a largely white neighborhood; exactly two black (Karen Johnson was one of them), four Latino, and seven Asian faces smile from the pages of my Hollywood High School yearbook. I grew up in a world in which the color flesh in crayons, Band Aids, or stockings meant an odd shade of sickly gray-pink. I knew, by the way, no nonhospitalized white person who was that color and, of course, I knew no Latino or black or Asian person whose flesh tone even came close.

I've always known I had this white culture, but the process of writing this book really drove it home. I spotted my culture first while deciding what questions to ask my research subjects. It came into view again as I watched my reactions to the anecdotes that came my way. I remember one story in particular. I read in Bruce Jacobs' book *Race Manners* about a black woman who because of the color of her skin was followed around an expensive department store by the store detective. Outraged, she finally went to the counter where she loudly demanded that the manager cancel her charge account.[5]

My first reaction to that woman's predicament was to put it in the same category as the tale of another woman who was also regularly followed by store detectives. That woman was middle-class and white. She was fond of wearing smocks with big pockets and routinely carried a large satchel-like purse. Because of how she dressed, it was common and reasonable for the local store detective to be suspicious and to keep a close eye on her every time she, and her giant purse, entered the store. In fact, this woman was no more apt to steal than the irate shopper from *Race Manners*, but she did have one weakness: a perverse sense of humor. As soon as she noticed the detective following her, she would feign put-

ting small items into her purse or pocket and got great pleasure in leading the poor man from department to department.

The woman with the silly sense of humor was my mother. For her, being followed by the store detective was a game; for the black woman, it was the height and depth of bias. The contrast between the two stories and my reaction to them helped me grasp how our own cultures distort our reactions to and understanding of the experiences of other people. I cannot be objective. But, then again, no one can. As you read, you will bring your own point of view and experience to the material. My reaction and how I treat an incident is from my perspective; you will read it from yours. The trick is to know that those perspectives exist.

ADVICE TO THE READER

Before you turn the page and launch into the body of this material, I suggest you do some preparation. Take a moment to think about what you are trying to accomplish. What is it that prompted you to pick up this book in the first place? Perhaps your goal will change as you move through the volume, but by starting with a specific result in mind, even a changeable one, you will be better able to maintain your focus. Also, before you read each chapter, look at the Reader's Guide in the Appendix for suggestions of conversations to have and issues to explore with each new topic.

I will say it again:

Reading this book is apt to make you feel the discomfort of self-discovery.

You will wince when one person's story of prejudice reminds you of your own and destroys any hope you had of hiding from your biases. No doubt you'll chafe under the task of responding to the various Exploration Point exercises scattered throughout the chapters. This discomfort may become so great that you will be tempted to put the book away. When the going gets too rough, remember that this book is filled with stories about people who are traditionally considered the good guys, who have admitted to having biases, faced up to them, and moved on to better relationships and better lives. You can be one of them.

As you read, sustain an optimistic attitude. As in any aspect of self-improvement, whether reducing bias or building self-esteem, optimism is a key to success. This is not a supernatural or superstitious notion; it is a fact. If we feel we cannot succeed, we quite rightly, and economically, reduce the amount of effort we put into finding creative solutions. If we wallow in the past, indulge in guilt, and listen to the naysayers who spout rhetoric about bias being a fatal and irrevocable flaw in human nature, we are doomed to defeat.

Let me start off on an optimistic foot by telling you about a black man who grew up in Louisiana in the 1950s and 1960s. His name is Tony Polk. As a young man, Tony went to a local hospital to give blood for an injured friend. Despite the generosity of his mission, Tony, because of his race, was forced to enter through the back door. Tony Polk and his contribution were not valued that day. Now they both are. Tony Polk currently holds the title of Diversity Director for the American Red Cross. There are, blessedly, thousands of other stories just like Tony's—stories of progress, and enlightenment, and optimism. Keep those in mind as you struggle with your own healing process.

Finally, this book is about each of us as individuals; it is not about the system. Yes, systems can be biased, but systems are created by individual human beings, sustained by individual action, and changed by individual creativity, courage, and influence. For that reason, this book talks about what each of us as individuals can and must do to reduce the bias within and around us. I challenge you to take personal, day after day, one-on-one responsibility for undertaking this task. There is no room for complaining about the system, your neighbor, your boss, your insensitive friends, affirmative action—pro or con—or the political climate. There is also no time to lose.

THE BASICS
OF BIAS

1

BIAS DEFINED AND MISDEFINED

What is a bias and why is there so much confusion
about what the word really means?

BIAS IS AN INFLEXIBLE BELIEF ABOUT A PARTICULAR KINSHIP GROUP

Which, if any, of these people are guilty of bias? I don't mean *might* be biased or *suspected* of bias, but absolutely, positively guilty?

- *Case 1:* Juan, a 50-year-old manager, had occasion to interview a woman named Nancy who, at the time of their meeting, was in her mid-20s. After the interview, Juan said to his boss, "I'd like to hire her, but we need someone willing to commit for the long run. Nancy has changed jobs four times since college. I hear that some people in her age group are that way, and she obviously fits the demographic."
- *Case 2:* It was the end of a long day at the diversity conference, and I was tired and ready to relax. Figuring that most of the people I knew would be in the hotel restaurant, I walked in hoping to hook up with a dinner companion or two. Upon entering the room, I was glad to see that it was filled with conference attendees. There was one problem, however: my friends were scattered between

two large tables. At one table, everyone was white; at the other, everyone was black. Because I knew the folks at both tables equally well, I was faced with a dilemma. Where do I sit? To be honest, my impulse as a white person was to go to the white table; a little more familiarity, a little more comfort. In the end, I gave into that impulse and took a seat at the table with the folks who looked most like me.

- *Case 3:* Ayana, an immigrant from Ethiopia, had been working at the department store for only three months. One morning, she was approached by a tall blonde woman who asked her to find a particular item in another size. Upon returning from her quest, Ayana walked up to the wrong customer and said that the size was unavailable. The woman looked at Ayana blankly; Ayana had mistaken one white woman for another.

- *Case 4:* When Harry heard his new neighbors speaking English with a Spanish accent, he assumed that because almost everyone else in his neighborhood had immigrated from Baja they were also from Mexico. In a gesture of welcome, he packaged up some homemade chocolate chip cookies, knocked on the door, and made awkward conversation beginning with, "I see you are from Mexico. How long have been in this country?" The couple was quick to point out that they were from Argentina not Mexico and, despite Harry's good intentions, were deeply offended. It took months to mend the rift.

- *Case 5:* Being a lifelong lover of the blues, Mary was thrilled to be invited to a concert presented by her favorite artists. Upon arriving at the venue, she made her way to her seat, which was next to the only white person in the audience. At the end of each concert, the musicians had a tradition of inviting the crowd to shake something white in the air as a symbol of solidarity and optimism. When the call came to perform this ritual, Mary realized that she had forgotten to bring the traditional white handkerchief, so without missing a beat she grabbed the man next to her and playfully started shaking him.

- *Case 6:* Gretchen listened patiently as the new Cambodian supervisor explained his design idea. She then nodded respectfully, said she'd think about it, and returned to her desk having understood very little of what the man had said. Gretchen later explained, "I didn't want to hurt his feelings, but Saru's accent was so heavy I just gave up. Besides, I'm sure it was a great idea; all Asians make wonderful engineers."

CASE 1: FLEXIBLE VERSUS INFLEXIBLE— JUAN WAS INNOCENT

Juan was innocent because what he felt about Nancy was not an "inflexible belief about a particular kinship group" but an observed fact about a specific individual. On the other hand, if prior to meeting her he had said of Nancy, "All Generation X employees change jobs a lot, I know that's the way Nancy will be," he would have been guilty of bias.

One reason some of you might have thought Juan was guilty is that the characteristic he ascribed to Nancy (changing jobs often) could, if applied inflexibly to all Generation Xers, indeed be a reflection of a bias against people born between 1961 and 1981. This confusion brings us to two key points that will help in your efforts to diagnose bias in yourself and others:

1. Biases are attitudes not behaviors. There is no such thing as a "biased action," only actions that to a greater or lesser degree of certainty hint at a biased attitude.
2. Just because a word or action is consistent with a biased attitude does not automatically mean it actually reflects a biased attitude.

It is probably in the realm of the clumsy, ignorant, and unlucky use of words that this erroneous connection between an action and a biased attitude is most often made. "Some of my best friends are . . . ," "You don't look Jewish," and "Gee, you're tall even for a black man, you ought to play basketball" are all statements that most certainly have been uttered by people whose very souls are riddled with bias. These statements are, admittedly, "consistent with" a biased viewpoint. As in a court of law, however, "consistent with" is not the same as "identical to" or "proof of."

CASE 2: "JUST LIKE ME"—I WAS INNOCENT

Being drawn to people like yourself is not necessarily a symptom of a biased attitude. If it were, the employees at one large hotel in Washington, D.C., would be in real trouble. Were you to look into a managers' meeting at this hotel, you would see a veritable United Nations of diversity: Latinos at one table, Vietnamese at another, Bosnians to the right, Iranians and Czechs and Poles scattered in clusters in the center of the room. Is it racism? It could be, but in this case it isn't. Being a nation in which segregation is a painful part of our history, we assume that the clustering of kinship groups is a sure sign that something is wrong. Do these groups feel uncomfortable with each other? Are they afraid or excluded or—our paranoia shouts—are they plotting something? It is time we bring a balance to this issue of being drawn to people like ourselves. We must learn when it is bias and when it is simple human comfort.

It is this desire for comfort and the wish to be with people with whom we identify that draws us to members of our own kinship group. That identification makes us feel that we have things to share, can get along, and probably have something to say to each other. We believe that members of our own group will understand our perspective and our needs. We also feel that if anything goes wrong between us, we will be able to figure out the problem and agree on a solution—after all, they are "just like me." This assumption of sameness is why we walk into a room filled with kinship groups of all descriptions and feel the urge to sit next to someone who reminds us of ourselves.

Another reason for this desire to be with people like us is the same reason that people dread public speaking: *fear of death.*

I'll let those of you who are afraid of presenting in front of a group sit with that a minute: *death.*

You know exactly what I mean and you probably feel a stirring of butterflies at the very thought of standing in front of an audience. Here's how this system, which feels like torture to some of you, works.

Public speaking involves exposing our intellect, our personality, and, come to think of it, our bodies to public evaluation. (Am I making you feel better?) Because of this vulnerability, performing badly in front of an audience results in what we experience as public humiliation. When this humiliation envelops us, our trembling subconscious spews up that most fundamental of fears: fear of exclusion from the group and the accompanying terror that, like a child abandoned in the woods, we will be deprived of the resources to survive. That is how deep the fear of public speaking can be and how primal the need is to belong to a kinship group.

By the way, there is nothing wrong with all this desire for solidarity nor does it make us any more prone to being biased. In fact, those of us who have a strong sense of kinship identity tend to be the very people who are most receptive to the ideas and input of other groups. This may seem paradoxical, but researchers agree. Joseph Ponterotto and Paul Pedersen say that having a healthy ethnic identity is essential to feeling good about other cultures:

Feeling confident in one's self, one's values, and one's culture increases, rather than decreases, the likelihood of being interested in and receptive to the cultures of others.[1]

A healthy *ethnic identity* or what might be called *group self-esteem* is merely a more global version of that darling of pop psychology: personal self-esteem. Personal self-esteem, like group self-esteem, is central to our ability and willingness to be open to what, and who, is new and different. As psychological theorist Nathaniel Branden puts it, "Self-esteem expresses itself in an attitude of openness to and curiosity about new ideas, new experiences, and new possibilities."[2] It's really very simple:

> *If we have a firm sense of our identity and our worth, we are not threatened by new ideas, fresh values, and unfamiliar ways of doing things.*

The more we believe our identity is valid, the less we fear that alternative ideas will threaten our image of who we are and what we have to contribute. The Exploration Point below will help drive this point home.

You probably wrote such adjectives as "adventurous," "interesting," and "confident." You most certainly recorded something like "receptive to new things and ideas" near the top of your list. This person is not obnoxious nor does he have a superiority complex. More likely, your chosen subject has such regard for and faith in his essential self that he realizes it is not necessary to appear or be perfect. This person can admit to incorrect decisions and then listen with an open mind to suggestions for improvement. He can genuinely consider alternative ways of doing things, listen to creative ideas from colleagues, explore suggestions for changes in policy—all without defensiveness or hostility. The person I mean has a sense of self so firm that alternative ideas are regarded as enhancements to a strong foundation rather than threats to the sense of self. If we agree that personal identity and self-esteem allow us to be more receptive to alternative ways of thinking, it follows that Ponterotti and Pedersen are right: Group

E *xploration*
P *oint*

Think of someone you know well who you believe has solid self-esteem. I don't mean a person who is arrogant, but someone who is, quite simply, comfortable in his or her skin. Other than a strong sense of self, what characteristics does this person have?

identity and group self-esteem make us more, not less, receptive to what other kinship groups have to offer.

CASE 3: "ALL WHITE PEOPLE LOOK ALIKE"— AYANA WAS INNOCENT

Confusing one member of a group for another is often erroneously thought to be symptomatic of bias. If we wanted to, we could jump all over Ayana, a woman who was not accustomed to being around white people, for mistaking one tall, blonde customer for another. The truth is, however, that her error is nothing more than an example of the truism that groups of things or people that are unfamiliar look alike to our untutored eye. Take wine for example, cabernet in particular. To me a cabernet is a cabernet is a cabernet. Each glass is like the next—a little pinker, a tiny bit sweeter—but any show I put on of knowing the difference is pure affectation. I have so little knowledge of wine in general and cabernets in particular that they all taste and look alike to me. To my son-in-law, however, a chef and wine enthusiast, the subtleties in taste, bouquet, and color are so varied that he would never mistake a California cabernet for one produced in France. The difference is that Josh is familiar with wines; his taste buds have met and made friends with so many individual cabernets that he can easily tell them a part. On the other hand, I could certainly give Josh a run for his money when it comes to noticing the differences between two antique desks or two Labrador retrievers.

If having difficulty distinguishing one individual from another makes a person biased, then the following incident reveals the dark truth that both my husband and I are in serious need of sensitivity training:

> When in Egypt some years ago, Tom and I were escorted to a light show at the pyramids by a driver who was most anxious to make our experience a pleasant one. As he dropped us off at the staging area, our escort went through lengthy and detailed instructions about where he could be found after the show and how we would recognize his cab. He then apologized for going on so long and said, "The problem is, you Americans all look alike. I'm afraid I'll take the wrong couple home." We laughed and admitted we had the same concern about him and appreciated the bright green flag of identification he had hung from the antenna of his car.

Apparently, even as sophisticated a man as Hippocrates had trouble telling individuals from unfamiliar groups apart. In his case, it was the nomadic Scythians who "all looked alike." I don't know how many Scythians ever ended up in Athens, but if they did, I'll bet they'd have had the same problem and a heck of a time picking Hippocrates out of a crowd of his fellow Greeks.

CASE 4: REASONABLE ASSUMPTION— HARRY WAS INNOCENT

In a perfect world, Harry would have asked first before assuming that his neighbors were from Mexico. He didn't, but that omission does not make him biased. Harry's only crime was drawing a reasonable conclusion and turning out to be wrong. I'm not sure I'd give his new neighbors the same break. The neighbors clearly felt that being mistaken for Mexican was an insult. This reaction points more to their own bigotry against Mexicans than it does to any biases Harry might have toward them.

Like Harry, Frank, the new doorman at David's New York apartment building, drew a reasonable conclusion when he assumed David was a deliveryman for a local Chinese restaurant. Consistent with security regulations and unfamiliar with the tenants, Frank asked David for identification before letting him into the building. David, a Chinese-American who was carrying a large bag of Chinese food, was furious and accused the doorman of racism. It is understandable that David was upset—he had, after all, worked hard to afford this apartment and buy all the expensive Chinese food he could eat. It is not, however, understandable that David accused Frank of bias; Frank's conclusion was a reasonable one in light of the fact that 95 percent of the apartments in his Upper West Side neighborhood were occupied by white Americans.

Frank made a mistake. One reason he made the error was that he had no time to consider his options. To avert a possible burglary, he had to act immediately; he had no opportunity to explore his heart and mind for the seeds of bias. Sometimes, like when walking down a dark alley, we simply have to play the odds that our assumption is correct. When Frank realized his error, he apologized profusely and let David go on his way. If he hadn't; if, after hearing David's explanation, Frank had persevered in his personal fiction that David did not belong there, the situation would have been different. At that point, it would have been a reasonable assumption to say that Frank was a bigot.

The difference between an error based on the available information and a bias is that the unbiased person who made the error is willing and able to change his mind in light of new evidence.

A word of caution (cases like Frank's aside):

It is unwise to act on every reasonable assumption that comes along.

If we did, we would be guilty of both legal and moral transgressions when we, for example, promote a man over a woman because of the possibility that the woman may quit to bear a child. There is, for example, no reasonable assumption more irrefutable than the fact that women are more likely to become pregnant than men, but that does not make it right, or legal, to act on the assumption that pregnancy will actually occur.

CASE 5: IN THE SPIRIT— MARY WAS INNOCENT

A good sense of humor, a sense of comfort with oneself, and a willingness to laugh at the forces that divide our society have nothing to do with bias. When I heard this story from the white person who had been so warmly embraced, I fell a little bit in love with Mary. I imagine you did too.

CASE 6: GUERILLA BIAS™— GRETCHEN WAS GUILTY

Poor Gretchen has the dubious distinction of being the only one of this bunch to be guilty of bias. She would probably be very upset to know this because Gretchen is one of the nicest of nice people. She has a good heart, never wants to hurt anyone's feelings, and likes to think well of others. The bad news for Gretchen, and for those around her, is that she is a carrier of a particularly dangerous species of bias: Guerilla Bias.

Defining Guerilla Bias

One reason Guerilla Bias is so dangerous is that it is difficult to spot and almost impossible to diagnose. This is because, like guerilla warfare in which the enemy is hidden within stands of lush foliage, Guerilla Bias lies concealed behind good intentions, kind words, and even thoughtful acts. In Gretchen's case, her so-called thoughtful acts included accepting Saru's ideas without really understanding them, assuming that his ideas were good just because he was Asian, and, finally, saying nothing about his poor communication skills.

Another reason that Guerilla Bias, despite its soft persona, is to be feared so much is that it is fueled by this particularly destructive premise: All women, emerging groups, people with disabilities, and those who are outside the so-called majority population are to some degree fragile, quick to explode, or in need of special treatment. We will see throughout the book several examples of the havoc that this patronizing assumption wreaks in the workplace; Gretchen's failure to help Saru with his communication skills is only the beginning.

The best way to understand Guerilla Bias is to compare and contrast it to more traditional notions of bias. Prior to the identification and naming of Guerilla Bias, biases were customarily divided into two categories. One category involves a conscious bias accompanied by blatantly biased behaviors. When Abby refused to hire Lester because she considered him fat and figured he must be lazy, she was guilty of a deliberate and observable bias against people who are overweight. When a person who is guilty of conscious bias is confronted, she is apt to defend herself by saying something like, "That's not a bias, that's just the way those people are."

The second type of bias is called *naive* or *passive* bias. In this case, the attitude is unconscious but still has a negative consequence that is observable by the target of that bias. An example of this is when Jack "forgot" to consider Carolyn for a promotion. Carolyn was highly qualified for the job; she was also, according to our culture's definition, overweight. As Jack later realized, he had dismissed her from consideration because of an unconsciously held bias that excessive weight is always a sign of laziness and self-indulgence. When a person who is guilty of naive bias is confronted, he is apt to come back with, "I didn't realize I was being biased. I apologize."

Guerilla Bias is similar to naive bias for the person is usually unaware that he or she is biased; it differs in that observers and those who are the target of the bias generally are also oblivious to what is going on. This is because the bias is disguised as a kindness. If confronted with a charge of being biased, the Guerilla Biased person probably replies with a heartfelt and sincere, "I'm not biased, I was just trying to be nice."

It is because of this latter statement that I have put so much emphasis on Guerilla Bias. Because it is so hidden and because it is held by so many of the nice people for whom this book is intended, it is important that we fully grasp its nature and ramifications.

Example of Guerilla Bias—Political Overcorrectness

Nowhere is Guerilla Bias, along with this misguided attempt at being nice, more neatly illustrated than in the lexicon and practice of political correctness. Each of these extreme examples is fueled by the biased myth that emerging groups are fragile and require special treatment:

- An expert witness in the O.J. Simpson murder trial insisted on referring to a hair found in the murderer's cap as "African-American" rather than the customary and fully acceptable scientific term, "Negroid."
- Coca-Cola fell into its own sticky vat of political correctness when an ad depicting couples watching a movie was criticized for its failure to include gay partners. Critics claimed that the absence of a gay couple denigrated the notion of same-sex relationships and that Coca-Cola should depict all kinds of couples in the future.[3] If this thinking were taken to its logical conclusion, every commercial would have to be peopled by dozens of couples of every conceivable ethnic, racial, and lifestyle combination. Imagine the casting nightmare.
- A promotional piece for the San Diego Padres' Diversity Day read, "Get free tickets if you come with a person of another color, religion, or ethnic group."[4]

This last example amounts to a 1990s version of the 1960s admonition to "invite a Negro to dinner." It is hard to imagine the purpose of such a thing except to make people feel virtuous about their treatment of emerging groups and maybe to soothe some ancient guilt.

Of course, not all efforts at increased sensitivity toward emerging groups are examples of Guerilla Bias. An important message, for example, was sent when we called a halt to the universal use of the pronoun he. After a period of awkwardness, like a child learning a new language, we began to give equal weight to the contributions of men and women, if not always in the culture at least in the language.

But now political correctness has gone overboard. Someone once paraphrased Mark Twain's attitude toward chastity by saying, "Political correctness is like chastity, it can be carried too far." Consisting initially of rules of language that dictated reasonable labels for emerging groups designed to communicate respect and equal power, political correctness gradually degenerated into ridiculous excesses that now serve only to bring criticism to more reasonably balanced efforts to reduce bias. What started out as a sensible adjustment has mutated into a form of Guerilla Bias.

Example of Guerilla Bias—Holding People to a Low Standard of Excellence

If a recent example of Guerilla Bias weren't so tragic, it would have the makings of a *Saturday Night Live* skit. It seems someone had the perverse wit to say that the New Jersey seat belt law that makes refusal to buckle up a primary offense is unfair to black drivers. The logic behind this contention is a classic example of how Guerilla Bias seduces us into holding certain groups to a low standard of behavior. Apparently black people fasten their seat belts less often than other groups so they would be prime targets for racist police officers who might use the unfastened belt as an excuse to harass black drivers. Granted racial profiling is a serious problem, but exempting a particular group from its legal obligation is not the solution; it is, in fact, an insult to a community whose members deserve as much as anyone else to survive automobile accidents. Making the black community an exception to a sensible and, might I add, lifesaving, law implies that black people are not as capable as others of complying.

In these and dozens of other ways, those who harbor Guerilla Biases invite members of emerging groups to measure down to their low expectations. This is an easy trap to step into and one in which many otherwise nice managers—managers like Gretchen—get snared.

Example of Guerilla Bias—The "Noble Savage"

Let me introduce you to another manifestation of Guerilla Bias. She is known as the "noble savage." You remember her from college. She's that mythical creature encountered by Western Europeans as they ventured around the globe. Made famous by French philosopher Jean-Jacques Rousseau in the 18th century, the noble savage concept glorified indigenous occupants of Africa and the New World as superior to Europeans in their closeness to nature and natural state. This attitude has again caught on, but this time it is in America's workplace rather than on foreign shores and has become manifested as Guerilla Bias. The concept has broadened slightly from the narrow idea that members of emerging groups are superior in their relationship to nature to more diffused notions of superiority. This kind of Guerilla Bias amounts to positive stereotyping and is seen in statements like "All blacks have rhythm," "All people with disabilities are brave," and Gretchen's "All Asians make wonderful engineers." Some say this type of prejudice creates no social problems. I disagree.

My friend and colleague Jean admits to having had, at one point in her life, a bit of a noble savage attitude. Jean acquired this perspective as a child growing up in the Arctic. Her exposure to Inuit children taught her to value a culture and way of being that was different from her own. In that sense, Jean's childhood was something to be envied. There was, however, a corollary teaching that served Jean less well. Her childhood experience left her enamored of anyone who is different and, by contrast, critical of those who are most like herself. She said to me, "The more like me someone is, the more she has to prove herself. When someone is different, I tend to give them a break." On the surface Jean's attitude seems relatively benign. What could possibly be wrong with cutting some slack for people who are different from us? In fact, it can be very wrong indeed.

Michael's story will help answer this question. Michael is a gay man who has a passion for baseball, 1950s' rock and roll, and Mexican food. As much as he loves these things, he has an equally strong aversion to art galleries and to talking about women's clothing, and he couldn't care less whether his couch matches the wallpaper. Michael, in short, conforms in no way to the popular bias: "All gay men are artistic." This came as a blow to Michael's boss who asked him to redecorate their small offices. The boss was angry when she learned that Michael had hired an interior decorator and couldn't understand why he hadn't just done it himself. Michael ended up looking bad, not because his boss held a negative view of gay men, but because she had the positive bias that Michael had an interest in redecorating the office himself and the skill to do the job.

Positive biases are as apt as negative ones to distort our perception of what a person is really like.

E *x p l o r a t i o n*
P *o i n t*

What makes Jean's attitude an example of Guerilla Bias?

A big problem with positive stereotypes and the noble savage is that each good thing we inflexibly believe about a group is invariably paired in our minds with something negative. Here are some examples:

- Those who praise Jews for their intellectual capabilities also tend to believe they are controlling.
- Those who see all Americans as ambitious are apt to also see them as greedy.
- Those who think Asians are good at sustaining intragroup harmony also tend to see them as too passive to be good managers.

I can think of few groups that we glorify more than the Irish, but our infatuation is a double-edged sword. Yes, we declare with a winsome smile, they are charming, but they are also childlike; yes, they are poetic, but they are also moody and temperamental. Everyone, of course, knows how creative the Irish are; how sad, we say, that this creative spirit leads them to drink.

Sound familiar? Most of us have negative biases, while still more of us have positive ones. The Exploration Point below will help you identify the ones that you hold.

Another problem with positive biases and the noble savage is that they, if taken to their logical conclusion, can lead to valuing an individual solely because of all the allegedly wonderful ways in which he is different. It was e.e. cummings who said:

> "To like an individual because he is black is just as insulting as to dislike him because he is not white."

Valuing diversity is a good thing. Valuing only diversity is shortsighted and cruel and smacks of the patronizing attitude of 18th-century white explorers who were infatuated with primitive rituals, exotic dress, and unfamiliar ways.

E *x p l o r a t i o n* **P** *o i n t*

1. What positive biases do you have? (Examples: "All gay men are creative," "All Asians are good at math," "All black men are good at sports.")
2. For each answer you gave to question one, see if there is a negative generality that accompanies it. (Examples: "Gay men are creative, but also emotional"; "Asians are good at math, but bad at verbal communication"; "Black men are athletic, but aren't very good at academics.")

IFS, BUTS, AND MAYBES

Defining bias is difficult; it involves a demoralizing glut of "yeses and nos," "ifs," "buts," and "maybes," each of which seems designed to drive us mad. *Yes,* being drawn to someone like yourself is normal; *no,* it should not be completely indulged. *Yes,* it is OK to make a reasonable assumption about an individual, *but* you are biased *if* you don't change your mind in the face of conflicting evidence. *Yes,* it is all right to make an honest mistake in current terminology, *but* we must make an effort to understand what bothers the people around you. *Yes,* some behaviors do not reflect a biased attitude, *but, maybe,* that behavior should be changed anyway.

The simplest way to cut through all this muddle is to think of a bias as the small voice inside each of us that, upon meeting a stranger, whispers, "I've known someone similar to you before so I know what you are like" or "I've heard about 'you people.'" Biases cause us to react, not to individuals but to a motley succession of stereotypes and caricatures. We no longer see the person as he is because the bias blocks our view. Bias is the gremlin that seduces even the kindest of us into patronizing the person in a wheelchair, graciously devaluing the contributions of our elders, and gently but oh-so-certainly making those who are different feel just a little bit less whole.

CHAPTER SUMMARY

- Behaviors and words are not biased; attitudes are biased. Actions that are consistent with bias may be inappropriate, but they do not automatically reflect a biased attitude.
- One of the key characteristics of a biased attitude is that it is inflexible.
- Because of the deep-seated need for group membership as a means of survival, there is nothing wrong with, nor biased about, being drawn to members of our own kinship group.
- When we are unfamiliar with a particular class of objects or people, individual units within that class tend to look alike. To mistake one member of an unfamiliar kinship group for another, for example, does not, unto itself, mean that we are biased.
- It is not bias to make a reasonable assumption based on available evidence. If, however, we later gather new information that con-

tradicts our original assumption and we fail to change our mind, then we are possibly guilty of bias.

- Even though reasonable assumptions are not automatically rooted in a biased attitude, it is still unwise to act on many of them.
- Guerilla Bias is a particular type of bias that is based on the premise that members of emerging groups, women, and people with disabilities are fragile and in need of special treatment. It is manifested in the workplace in many ways, including in the failure to properly coach members of emerging groups.

2

CAREFULLY TAUGHT: HOW BIAS IS LEARNED

CHAPTER FOCUS QUESTION

How do we learn biases and why are they so deeply ingrained?

It was a subtle message and if its impact had not been so sad, you could almost say it was gentle. There was no violence, no foul words hurled like weapons, just a shadowy teaching hidden beneath the stern admonition not to share her Coke with the son of the black housekeeper.

That is how the seed of bias got imbedded deeply inside the fertile soil of Joan's adolescent psyche. It was planted far more subtly than was Rose's belief that "All Mexicans are destructive." That grew out of one horrifying night when two drunk teenagers from her all-Mexican neighborhood tried to break into her house. She was alone, her phone was disconnected, and she was, understandably, terrified. The experiences of these two women were different, but the end result was the same: they were both contaminated with a negative bias toward an entire population of people.

Carlos, who was beaten into life in a wheelchair by two white thugs, is an example of the damage that this contamination if allowed to fester can do. At the sentencing hearing, Carlos asked the offenders, "How did you learn to hate?" I don't know how or even if the young men answered

Carlos's question, but I have a fair idea of what the answers would have been. Perhaps their hate was acquired via behavior modeled by a hateful and frightened parent, possibly it grew out of one bad experience, or maybe it was spread by a media so hungry for sensationalism that it painted every black man as someone to be hated and feared and defended against.

The purpose of this chapter is to help us understand why biases are so easily learned and how that learning actually takes place. The discussion includes the following topics:

- Why we are so vulnerable to acquiring biases
- How biases are learned from our parents and experience
- The role of culture and media in spreading biases
- The mechanisms that keep bias alive in the face of contradictory evidence

IMMUNE DEFICIENCY: WHY WE CONTRACT BIASES

You would think that human attitudes, like physical traits, would be subject to the laws of evolution with the fittest and most functional thriving and the least functional—attitudes like bias—shriveling like a useless appendix. As it turns out, evolution may be great at ridding us of gills and webbed feet, but it is remarkably poor at bringing about the extinction of bias. On the contrary, it seems as if human beings are afflicted with an immune deficiency when it comes to catching the bias bug. We are receptive, even eager, to develop biases despite the fact that they put us in little better than a dream state in which we misjudge and misread, and, as a result, mismanage many of our relationships.

The reason we are so vulnerable to acquiring biases is that deep down we believe they benefit us in some way. Most of these benefits aren't worth the trade-off in damaged lives and disrupted workplaces, but we fail to realize that at the time of our initial exposure. We'll take a closer look at these alleged benefits later on, but for now, let's examine just one: the illusion that biases magically imbue us with the ability to anticipate the attitudes, character, and behaviors of people different from ourselves. In other words, we like to think that our biases enable us to predict the unpredictable.

This desire to predict the unpredictable is an ancient and primitive urge, one which has given rise to all manner of ritual and superstitious thinking; bias, in that sense, is magic. Like magic, bias is illogical. If you have any doubt about how pervasive magical thinking is, admit that you feel just a bit more confident on the golf course when wearing that "winning" shirt or, like one renowned golfer admits, carrying two "lucky" tees in your left-hand pocket. Notice the tightening in your stomach when you encounter a ladder straddling the sidewalk. Do you bravely walk under it or do you reveal your superstitious nature and your desire to magically control your future by stepping around the ladder into busy traffic?

These feelings are similar to those that give rise to bias, not only because they are illogical, but also because they are driven by fear. Let's face it, human beings are fundamentally afraid. We are afraid of death, we are afraid of physical pain and loss of self, we are even afraid of being afraid. Above all, we are afraid of the uncontrollable and the unpredictable. It is this fear that animates—and propels—all of our magic and most of our biases.

In some ways, life is scarier today than it was in the past and, thus, our susceptibility to bias is greater than ever before. We are constantly immersed in the activity and distractions of modern living; life has become too complicated and that is frightening. William James described his modern 19th-century world as a cacophony of "blooming, buzzing, confusion." The 21st century is even more "buzzing," because of the increased human diversity we encounter every day. We also live at a time when knowledge is doubling every 18 months. To make matters worse, one quarter of that information will be obsolete in ten years. No wonder we are afraid.

All this complexity and the resulting anxiety renders us desperate to sort out and tidy up the cacophony of knowledge and people that make up our everyday world. Unfortunately, the unit of chaos that we most want to sort out is that which is the least "sortable": the behaviors and characteristics of diverse human beings. Because bias is an everything-in-its-place mentality, too many of us choose bias as the software with which to do that sorting. The problem is that everything in its place might be fine when organizing socks and underwear, but it sure works poorly with human beings.

The categories our biases create make it harder, not easier, to understand the variety of people around us.

It is difficult for even the best of us to resist the temptation to create categories. This is because we just don't have the time to research every truth about every person we meet. We are forced, or feel we are forced, to make inferences, to use educated guesses, and to respond to and act on first impressions based on what bias scholar Gordon Allport calls "rough and ready rubrics."[1]

We crave anxiety-relieving information and we want it immediately. That urgency becomes the controlling force that outweighs our desire for accuracy and precision. Nothing is more inaccurate, but, admittedly, more available, than human bias. Like a drug that provides an initial high followed by depression, biases at first make us feel more secure only to create more anxiety when their inaccuracies are exposed. Despite the inadequacies of the tool, however, most of us feel more comfortable with the counterfeit certainties of bias than with the ambiguity of real life.

INITIAL INFECTION:
TRIBAL LEADERS AND EXPERIENCE

Tribal Leaders as Carriers of Bias

Many of us grew up in homes that were veritable petri dishes of the bias virus. We lived each moment watching, listening, experiencing in an atmosphere infected with biased messages and subtle or not-so-subtle examples of distorted vision. It may not be fashionable these days to blame parents for our faulty thinking, but when it comes to bias, we must lay the responsibility firmly in Mom and Dad's overburdened laps.

Parents are the most powerful people we know during our formative years. They are our tribal leaders and because they are the primary force that guides us, we believe what they say. If parents are open-minded (read unafraid), that is great. Children of open-minded parents learn to be in the moment and evaluate each person as she comes along; they have no psychological need to divine the nature or intentions of individuals according to the group to which they belong. If, on the other hand, our parents are carriers of bias, we become infected not only with specific biases but with the notion that biased thinking in general is an effective approach to solving life's problems.

Of all the biases our parents teach us, it is the subtle ones, such as the Guerilla Biases™ we discussed in the last chapter, that are the most dangerous. If you have a parent who is blatantly biased, whose idea of a good time on a Saturday night is to burn a cross on someone's lawn, at least the message is clear. Because the bias is obvious, we—the children—can intellectualize it, name it, and target it for extinction. On the other hand, most parents provide a gentler primer that, paradoxically, is harder to unlearn. Take my friend Carol, for example. Carol has only the vaguest memory of the racist comments her black father used to make about the white friends she brought home and, as such, was unaware until middle age of the bias against whites with which she was infected. Then there is Lee, a nice, but infected, man who only recently remembered that his grandfather admonished him not to say "Yeah" because that was "Injun talk." For Rhonda it was the way her mother imperceptibly lowered her voice when identifying a new acquaintance as Jewish. Have you ever experienced these kinds of messages?

E *x p l o r a t i o n*
P *o i n t*

Think back to your childhood and try to recall a subtle message of bias that might have been imparted to you by your parents. What is your first memory of hearing this message?

As you undertake this exercise, you may find that not only was the message subtle, it may also have been contradictory or ambiguous. My father was what you might call an ambivalent racist. In that role, he supplied me with just such a mixed message. For some time, when he was first in Hollywood struggling to establish his career, he stood on a skid row street corner with men of all descriptions hoping for any manual labor that might come his way. Never during this period did a word of bias or hatred or even fear come out of his mouth toward his fellow laborers. On the other hand, years later when I was the victim of an armed robbery, his first question was, "Were they black?" This question contradicted my father's obvious respect for his skid row chums. Because the message I received was inconsistent, it was difficult to refute, difficult to cleanly label as "bigotry," and, therefore, hard to target for extinction.

Experiences as Catalysts for Bias

My first experience with anyone foreign took place in the hills of Hollywood, California, when I was ten years old:

> Every few weeks a Chinese peddler would visit our neighborhood offering his services as a knife sharpener. My memory is that the man was short and stooped and had curled and yellowed fingernails at least as long as his hands. I often wonder about the accuracy of this memory and how exotic and mysterious a being he really was. What I do know for sure is that he

materialized periodically towing (or was it pushing?) a creaking wooden cart laden with a primitive stone sharpener and dozens of knives and that his strident street-vendor cry had the unfamiliar lilt of Chinese-accented English. It was that cry that would inspire my sister and I to squeal and scurry into the backyard where we would collapse in gales of jittery giggles.

Those "jittery giggles" belied the discomfort Susan and I felt every time this exotic figure rounded the corner of our street. This discomfort, in turn, triggered the bias: "Foreigners, especially if they are from the Far East, are to be feared and avoided."

Scary though they were, these occasional visitations were relatively benign compared to the kinds of experiences that usually create biases. More often than not, biases are surgically implanted through one negative and painful encounter. One reason negative events create the most firmly held biases is that anything negative or frightening, if taken to its logical conclusion, threatens our survival and, therefore, gives rise to strong emotions. As Gordon Allport puts it, " . . . intense emotional feelings have a property of acting like sponges. Ideas, engulfed by an overpowering emotion, are more likely to conform to the emotion than to objective evidence."[2] Allport's "ideas" are our biases.

We can understand how this works by examining what is called *terror management theory*. Terror management theory suggests that fear causes us to turn to those whom we think of as our own and reject those who are outside our group.[3] When we combine this dynamic with what we know about the tendency to exaggerate the difference between our own kinship group and others, we see why one threatening or otherwise negative experience with an out-group member not only implants a bias into our trembling subconscious but amplifies our perception of difference. Picture a five-week-old puppy tentatively venturing out from its mother. Startled by the hiss of a cat, the dog whirls around and scurries back to the warmth of its pile of littermates—her own version of a human kinship group. That puppy, particularly if it is at a formative period in its social development, is in danger of forever assuming that all cats are dangerous and, to make the fear still worse, of having an exaggerated idea of how different cats are from dogs. The puppy becomes biased.

Geraldo probably wouldn't want to hear it, but he is just like that puppy. Because of one bad experience with one passenger, this San Antonio cabdriver will not give rides to young black men. Even Ron, who always thought of himself as a tolerant sort, refuses to hire a female assistant because of the false sexual harassment charges the last one brought against him. Both men have allowed the fear they experienced on one occasion to color their perception of an entire population of people.

There is another reason that negative experiences often give rise to bias: Many of us are fascinated with drama, and the more negative and frightening that drama, the more we like it. Why else would the media be so successful when it reports and exaggerates stories of violence and hatred? The answer is that most of us like the illusion of a little danger in our lives. Anthropologist Jennifer James addresses this issue when she says that we "love the feeling of being in battle, [we are] hunters and warriors at heart." Danger, she argues, gives us an adrenaline rush and the opportunity to prove our cunning and our strength.[4] It is the craving for this rush that tempts us to transform any negative encounter into a belief in an ongoing threat; we do this by adopting a negative bias about the group involved. Negative bias becomes, therefore, a device that allows us to believe we are still conquering the frontier, girding for battle, or, at the least, that we are just a little bit braver than our daily routines allow us to demonstrate.

THE VIRUS SPREADS

The Impact of Culture

Once we are infected, either through our parents or by experience, each of us becomes a carrier of the bias bug. This contagion can happen in any environment, but it takes place most readily in cultures that are cordial hosts for this particular strain of disease. One way in which cultures manifest this hospitality is by tolerating, at least to some degree, the open expression of biased attitudes. This is one reason that biases are destructive no matter who holds them. It is tempting to say, for example, that a woman's bias against other women doesn't count as much as a man's or that a Chinese person's bias against the Japanese is OK because they are both Asian. This logic, however, crumbles when we realize that tolerating anyone's bias creates a climate in which the rest of us can feel that ours must be acceptable too. When this happens, bias gradually becomes a transgression akin to cheating on one's taxes and we begin to rationalize our prejudices by saying, "Everybody does it so why shouldn't I?"

Can you, for example, think of a better excuse for white racism than the colorism found in the black community? Take the case of the Jamaican cabdriver who, to this day, laments the lost love of his youth:

The driver spoke to me with obvious emotion of how his fiancée had abruptly called off the wedding, given no explanation, and moved to another city leaving no forwarding address. Recently, on a trip back to his hometown, my heartbroken friend discovered why his fiancée had left: His grandfather had told the woman that she, because of the dark color of her skin, was not, and never would be, welcomed into the family.

As I sat in the backseat listening to this tale of woe, I fantasized how this story could affect someone who was cultivating a bias against black people. First, I imagine, such a person would feel a compassionate bond with the driver over the shared agonies of lost love and thwarted romance. There would also be agreement with the grandfather's position and with that agreement would come pleasure at having been handed a cup full of fertilizer for her budding bias. "Yes," the biased passenger might think, "I can see why the grandfather would do that. After all, he needs to maintain the purity and status of his family. Sounds sensible to me."

Another reason that biases held by one group can perpetuate them in others is what psychologist Daryl Bem calls *semantic generalization.* Semantic generalization is a fancy phrase for a simple idea: If you hear a bias long enough, you begin to believe it.[5] In this process, just hearing enough people say something negative or positive about a group makes it real. If enough people hear Jan refer to her Japanese peers as "hot off the boat," or Tony call Italians "dagos," it isn't necessary to have had any contact with Japanese immigrants or Italians to begin to agree with these assessments. It also doesn't matter that Jan is of Japanese ancestry or that Tony is Italian, the contagion is just as virulent.

The Impact of the Media

No force, however, spreads bias more effectively than the media. Because of its passion for exaggerating reality, the media is particularly qualified for this task. It presents isolated instances as trends, distorts images and groups, and, worst of all, bombards us with inflated dangers. Unless the threat is an earthquake or hurricane, these dangers are inevitably linked to some group of human beings. Inevitably too, the actions of these groups, whether they are inner-city youths or Arab Muslims or fundamentalist Christians, are depicted in the most brilliant colors. There is, after all, no story unless there is drama and what is more dramatic than violence and threat and danger? You know what they say about the media, "If it bleeds, it reads."

The effect of this verbal and visual hyperbole is that we become unable to separate the real threat from a sound bite. I remember watching a video clip during the 1992 Los Angeles riots depicting a group of kids gleefully pilfering television sets, radios, and VCRs from a local discount store. Every time I saw that piece of film, I became angry. I became angry because I know that another clip exists that shows many of those very same kids being forced by their parents to take their ill-gotten loot back to the local churches. None of us saw the positive footage—it just wasn't interesting enough to air—so we were left with the impression that all kids in South Los Angeles are thieves with irresponsible parents. Another bias was born.

THE PROGNOSIS

The bias virus is remarkably hardy. One reason for this toughness is that most of us just can't stand being wrong and will do almost anything to prove our biases correct. Psychologists call this process *belief perseverance* and talk a lot about the numerous mind games we play to keep our biases alive. For example, we:

- Ignore or forget information that does not support our bias.
- Give extra weight and credence to information that validates our bias.
- Rationalize and distort what we see to make it conform to our bias.
- Act on our bias in a way that allows it to become a self-fulfilling prophecy.

Once we go through all this effort to convince ourselves of the truth of our biases, things really get interesting:

The more we believe the bias to be true, the more we think of it as desirable.

As soon as we decide the bias is desirable, our mind redoubles its efforts to locate and remember any evidence of how right we are no matter how tenuous. This result is:

The more we think it is desirable, the more we think it is true.[6]

It is because of this stubbornness that once a bias is born, it is tough, but not impossible to eradicate, as you will see in the following pages. The rest of this book is devoted to providing the knowledge and skills needed to bring about this eradication and minimize the destructive influence of bias in our lives and in our workplaces.

CHAPTER SUMMARY

- One reason we learn biases so readily is that they provide us with the desired illusion that we can predict the behavior and character of people different from ourselves.
- Many of our initial lessons in bias come from our parents who expose us to subtle and sometimes ambiguous biases that, because they are so subtle, can be difficult to identify and defeat.
- Another way we learn biases is through experiences that frighten us into connecting more firmly with our own group while forming negative associations with the objects of our fear.
- One rarely mentioned reason for acquiring negative biases is that some people like the stimulation and challenge that comes from living in a dangerous world.
- Inflexible generalities thrive best in cultures in which biased thinking is regarded as acceptable. This is one reason that biases must be condemned regardless of who holds them.
- Once we acquire a bias, we strive to hold on to it by distorting any contradictory evidence that comes our way. We also give greater weight to experiences that support our biases and take actions that cause them to become self-fulfilling prophecies.

THE VISION RENEWAL PROCESS

"It's hopeless," Jim told me. "We can't stop bias. All we can do is wait for this generation to die off and a new one to come along." "Fine," I was tempted to reply, "then let's just give up and forget the whole thing." Even as erudite a man as Edward R. Murrow believed we can never rid ourselves of biases, only recognize them and learn to work around them. Fortunately, both Edward R. Murrow and Jim are wrong. Of course, some people refuse to change, but for each of those, there are millions who, given the right circumstances and enough determination, can correct their distorted vision and see the world and its people more clearly.

Those who argue that biases can't be fixed say that they are an intrinsic part of human nature (whatever that is) and, therefore, impossible to eradicate. Every time I hear the phrase *human nature* or *We're only human,* my hackles go up. To say that an attitude is *only human* implies that to be human is to be incapable of change; it connotes that there's not a darn thing we can do to improve ourselves or our attitudes. I am more optimistic than that. I believe that through awareness, knowledge, and plain old-fashioned effort, we can, at the very least, reduce our biases to the point where they have a minimal influence on our lives and work.

For any change to occur, however, we must break what is essentially a nasty habit of thought. If you think about it, that is what bias is: It is a conditioned way of thinking created by imagined necessity and perpetuated by repetition. To break the bias habit, we need to undertake a program of awareness, exploration, and practice. Part Two provides a mechanism for facilitating this process. It is called the Visual Renewal Process (VRP), and it will help you become aware of your biases and guide you step-by-step through the stages of ridding yourself of their influence. It will also provide you with tools for helping those around you do the same. Essentially, what the VRP does is freeze-dry each target bias by taking the emotional juice out of it, thus reducing it to an inert lump that can be grabbed and tossed out of your thinking and out of your life.

This may sound complicated, but the Process is relatively straightforward. The reason it works so well and is so easy to understand is that the VRP embodies a natural progression from one step to the next. These steps are so logical that you may have already passed through some of them without realizing it. For instance, you probably can recollect previously held biases that have slowly dissolved through the years—no major revelations, no dramatic conversion experience, just a gradual fading away and an accompanying clearing of vision. If you were able to go back and observe that slow dissolution, you would no doubt find that, unknown even to yourself, you passed through several of these steps.

Not only is the VRP logical, it also allows those who are naturally further along to start at a later point. For example, Step One ("Become Mindful of Your Biases") describes how to become aware of your biases. Perhaps you already are aware and can move on to decide which biases you want to target for extinction (Steps Two and Three). Maybe you have already chosen which biases to attack, so you can plunge into the next step of dissecting your biases to reveal their weaknesses (Step Four: "Dissect Your Biases").

Some of you will find parts of the Process easier than others. This is because one of the strengths of the strategy is that it employs not only the intellect but emotion and experience as well. Very few of us are able to work equally well in all three arenas. It is tempting to suggest you just skip those steps that don't come naturally, but that would be a mistake because it just might be those very steps that are, because of their difficulty, the ones you need the most. This is where courage comes in. It would be naive to say that it doesn't take courage to examine the damage that our biases have caused, to question the veracity of some of the people we have most admired, or to broaden our definition of the group to which we belong. It would, however, also be naive to say that we can build productive workforces and satisfying lives without getting our biases under control.

No matter what your learning style, what is true for all of us is that the Vision Renewal Process will, at some point, feel a little threatening. When this happens, take comfort from knowing that success does not require a complete mutation of who you are, a change of personality, or even a shift in fundamental values. It does require honesty and effort and a willingness to face your fears, have new experiences, and break a destructive habit of thought.

3

STEP ONE:
BECOME MINDFUL OF
YOUR BIASES

CHAPTER FOCUS QUESTION

How can I become aware of my biases to target them for extinction?

Dostoyevsky, in *Notes from the Under-ground,* said of our penchant for self-deception:

> Every man has reminiscences which he would not tell to everyone but only his friends. He has other matters in his mind which he would not reveal even to his friends, but only to himself and that in secret. But there are other things which a man is afraid to tell even to himself, and every decent man has a number of such things stored away in his mind.

One category of Dostoyevsky's sequestered things is our biases, our secret beliefs of how we feel about other groups of people. I agree with Dostoyevsky that fear is the primary cause of this secrecy. The fear that prevents us from admitting bias is that of having to acknowledge, even to ourselves, that we may not be quite as nice as we, and others, like to think we are. Until we overcome our dread of looking like bad people, or at least like less good people, we will be unable and unwilling to acknowledge our biases, name them, and target them for extinction.

Carrie, a nurse supervisor at a large medical center, was one of the afraid. In her case, fear prevented her from admitting that she had a bias against Filipinos. The result: litigation.

> I'm still not convinced that a discrimination suit was warranted, but I'll admit I did look at the Filipino nurses differently. I didn't realize it at the time, but since I knew their training was not like ours, I figured it was inferior. Every time they made the slightest error, I'd exaggerate it in my mind and get all over them. No wonder they felt I was treating them unfairly. I was. At the time I guess I just didn't want to admit that I was capable of bias.

Well, Carrie can rest easy. The good news is that being guilty of bias does not make her, or any of us, bad people. Bias, as we have seen, is a way of coping with a complex, stressful, and ever-changing world. Yes, these personal fictions are bad because they block our ability to see others accurately, but most of the people who hold them are multifaceted human beings complete with virtues and sins and everything in between. What would make a biased person bad, or at least unwise, is the refusal to identify the bias and accept responsibility for getting it under control.

POSITIVE ID

Identifying our biases is a matter of facing reality—painful, embarrassing reality. I had just such a reality check recently. It would be convenient to pretend that this incident took place years ago, long before I took up the work of bias reduction, but if I did, I'd be lying. Because this book is about telling the truth, that would be dirty pool. In fact, the incident happened in the fall of 2001. You'd think at that stage of the game I would have known better:

> The target of my bias was a black man named Louis who had recently begun dating a white friend of mine. In an effort to make Louis more comfortable in our social circle, I chatted with him at a couple of parties; no response. I tried bringing up subjects that might interest him; still nothing. I kept making excuses for Louis, saying things like "He must be uncomfortable," "Let's give him a chance," "We need to try harder." My daughter, never one to keep her opinions to herself, I am proud to say, finally asked, "Mom, would you try this hard if he were white?"

At first I resisted Shea's criticism, but eventually had to admit that I was expecting less of Louis than I would if he shared my culture and my race. As it turns out, Louis lacked not only social graces but several other virtues as well, which I would have concluded weeks earlier if I hadn't been so busy holding him to a low standard because of the color of his skin. I had to face it, I was guilty of the very same Guerilla Bias™ of which I accuse others.

In this case, it was my daughter who helped me face my guilt. Most of the time, however, we are on our own and that's what this chapter is all about: providing the tools to identify your own biases. You will be glad to hear that becoming aware of most biases is a straightforward process—no shrinks, no psychotherapists need apply. It is a matter of practicing the art of observation and evaluation:

- Observe your thoughts.
- Analyze your thoughts.
- Measure the emotional content of your thoughts.
- Observe your attitudes toward human difference.

You will notice that "observe your behaviors" is not on this list. Nowhere are you asked to record the number of times you failed to call on someone in a meeting, used a slightly inappropriate term, or decided against promoting a member of an emerging group. The reason for this apparent omission is that—with the exception of extreme acts of hatred and discrimination—behavior is the circumstantial, and notoriously unreliable, evidence of bias detection.

STRATEGY 1: OBSERVE YOUR THOUGHTS

All biases, even the most deeply subconscious ones, periodically appear in the form of a thought. It is our job to examine that thought to see what it tells us about our hidden beliefs. This means we need to watch what we think. "How can I watch my thoughts?" you may be asking. "I am my thoughts, there would be no 'me' without them and if there is no 'me,' there is no one home to do the watching."

These are understandable questions considering the nature of our culture in which thought and intellect are highly prized, but the truth is, we are not what we are thinking. There is a "you," an awareness that lies behind your thoughts that is capable of observing and chronicling them as they rush by. Give it a try, right this minute. Watch the thoughts that are coming into your mind. Maybe they go something like this:

What is this woman talking about? I thought this was a diversity book and all of a sudden we're talking about mind control or something. . . . Better remember to call Jake about the game Saturday morning. . . . I wonder where she's going with this stuff. . . . Wish I hadn't been so rough on Wong at the meeting last week, I know he's trying his best. . . . Wonder if he really feels comfortable here. . . . So glad Gladys liked the doll I brought her from New York, sure am lucky to have a daughter like her. . . . Hope I can get the raise so we can put her in the private school. . . . Wonder if this book will really teach me anything about diversity, sure hope so. . . .

And on they roll seemingly into infinity: thoughts, ruminations, speculations, worries, fantasies, ideas, reminiscences. Thought is alternatively fun and horrible, and irritating and entertaining. It is also a wonderful tool for survival and creativity. Thought is not, however, who we are.

We've all watched our thoughts before. Have you ever, for example, taken a word-association test in which you were asked to say the first thing that comes to mind when you hear the word *cat,* or *house,* or *airplane.* You probably responded with *dog, home,* and *fly* (or, possibly, *bad food*). When you notice and then say the word that pops up, you are watching your thoughts. That's all there is to it, we do it all the time; it's just that when it comes to something more substantial than a parlor game—like becoming mindful of an attitude—we lose sight of how simple and familiar the process is.

The next Exploration Point provides a chance to watch and record thoughts that might be clues to your biases. The exercise consists of a list of kinship groups to which I want you to react. (*Stop!* Don't look at the list until you are ready to do the exercise). As you read each item, jot down the first thought that comes to mind regarding a characteristic of that group. There are just a few rules you'll need to follow:

- Take only five seconds to come up with your response. If you can't think of anything by then, move on to the next category.
- Try to decipher quickly if the thought that emerges is what you really feel or if it is a stereotype held by the culture at large that came to mind merely because you have heard it so often. If you are certain that it is a general cultural bias and not your own, don't put it down. If you have any doubt at all, go ahead and record it.
- Resist the urge to edit your response.

Most important, do not be afraid of your answers for no one will see the list but you. Also, don't jump to conclusions about what the thought means. The thought by itself may or may not actually reflect a bias. We won't know that until we examine it further.

Are there any categories for which you were unable to come up with an answer? If so, good for you! This is probably the only test you will ever take in which a blank answer is the right answer. The harder it was for you to quickly think of a characteristic of a group, the less likely it is that you hold a bias against them.

The next step in the process is to take the practice of watching your thoughts out into the real world. There, instead of a list, you will have a variety of real people to react to. See the Exploration Point below.

I was around, fortunately (or unfortunately) for him, when my husband, Tom, had his own real-world moment of bias mindfulness. We had been shopping in downtown San Diego and had just returned to our car when it happened:

> Tom was opening the driver's side door just as a car drove up and stopped at the corner. When he turned to look, he saw four young black men in an automobile so derelict you couldn't help but wonder

E *x p l o r a t i o n* **P** *o i n t*

Write down the first characteristic that comes to mind as you read each of these categories. Feel free to add to the list any groups about which you have strong feelings.

An older person

A blind person

A Muslim

A fundamentalist Christian

A black person

A 50-year-old white male

A 23-year-old white woman

A person in a wheelchair

A person from Vietnam

A gay man

A female engineer

E *x p l o r a t i o n* **P** *o i n t*

For the next two weeks, notice and write down the first thought that comes to mind when you encounter someone from another kinship group. (Examples: What is the first thing you think of when you see an Arab name on an application? What hunches rise from your belly when you learn that your colleague is gay? What conclusions do you draw when you see a skin color, the slant of an eye, or a Phi Beta Kappa key dangling on a chain?)

how it was still running. To my husband's irritation, all four windows were rolled down and music was blasting out of the car as if to say to the neighborhood, "We're here and this is what we like. You'd better like it, too." When Tom saw the car and the young men and heard the music, he looked at me and said with ill-disguised irritation, "I really HATE that rap music."

Because of a stop sign on the corner, the car lingered within earshot for a few seconds and we were forced to listen to more of the song that they were playing. As we did, we began to hear, "Chicago, Chicago, that wonderful town . . ."; the singer was Frank Sinatra. These four youths were driving the streets of our town paying homage to my husband's favorite entertainer the day after he had died. My husband, however, was unable to hear the music he loved so much because his bias—his expectation—distorted his senses. All he could hear was the rap music that his bias told him to expect.

When Tom and I got in the car, the diversity trainer in me took over and the poor man was forced to listen to a treatise about what a great opportunity this was for him to become aware of his bias: "Lower-income black men—especially those who like their music loud and drive derelict cars—all listen to rap music." Would that be a reasonable guess if my husband were asked on a quiz show about the musical tastes of various groups? Sure. On the other hand, would that answer apply absolutely and without a doubt to every low-income black man in the city? Of course not.

My request to Tom that day (and to myself every day) was that the next time he jumps to a hasty conclusion about anyone's taste in music or any other characteristic for that matter, he watch the thought as it pops into his mind and label it for what it probably is: a puff of smoke drifting up from a deeply buried and distorting bias.

STRATEGY II: ANALYZE YOUR THOUGHTS

Watching our thoughts is important, but it is merely the evidence-gathering stage of our investigation; the next step is to examine that evidence to determine what it really means. One way to do this is to look at each initial reaction that you have chronicled and ask yourself this question: Would I feel the same way about the meaning of an incident if the actor were of a different kinship group? Here are some examples:

- A female executive shouts and pounds the table when speaking of the underhanded tactics of a competitor. You turn to the person next to you and whisper, "She sure is getting hysterical."

  Ask yourself this question: "If the executive had been a man rather than a woman, would I have still thought he was hysterical or would I have assumed he was justifiably angry?" If your answer is no—you would not have thought he was hysterical—you just might have a bias that tricks you into believing that women are more apt than men to get hysterical when under pressure.

- A male executive makes a comment about a woman that you consider evidence of sexism.

  Ask yourself this question: "If the comment had come from a woman and was about a man rather than from a man about a woman, would I still have thought it was sexist?" If your answer is no, you just might have a bias that tricks you into believing that all men are sexist or at least that men are more likely than women to have a chauvinistic attitude.

- A black clerk in the grocery store is moving very slowly as she counts out the change for the customer in front of you. You become impatient and think, She sure is slow; I wonder where they get these people.

  Ask yourself this question: "If the clerk had been white rather than black, would I still have thought she was slow or would I have seen her as fastidious?" If your answer is no, you just might have a bias that tricks you into believing that black people are slow and lazy.

- A colleague with a heavy foreign accent presents a proposal for a new product at the monthly meeting. You know he is a good employee, but you don't like his ideas very much.

  Ask yourself this question: "If my colleague didn't have an accent, would I have liked his idea better?" If your answer is yes, you just might have a bias that tricks you into believing that people with accents are less intelligent.

- You are a police officer who sees a black man make an otherwise safe lane change without signaling. You pull him over for this minor violation.

  Ask yourself this question: "If the driver of the vehicle had been white, would I still have pulled over the car?" If your answer is no, you just might have a bias that tricks you into believing that black people are prone to crime and need to be more carefully investigated than white people.

I learned recently of an incident similar to these that took place in a department store. It involved a black woman and a (very) small pocket-knife that dropped out of her purse when she was looking for her wallet. The sales associate became alarmed when she saw the knife and called security. The investigation that accompanied the (understandable) discrimination suit that followed revealed that calling security had a whole lot more to do with the fact that the customer was black than with that (again) (very) small knife. Had the staff person been going through the Vision Renewal Process, she might have stopped before calling security and asked herself: "Would I feel threatened by this woman if she were white?" If her answer had been "No," she might very possibly have a bias against black women.

STRATEGY III: MEASURE THE EMOTIONAL CONTENT OF YOUR THOUGHTS

The second step in determining if your thoughts are evidence of bias is to see how much emotion is attached to them. The more emotion, the more likely it is that the thought reflects a biased attitude. Both Andy and Thomas, for example, gave a negative answer when asked for their opinion about the gay men with whom they work. Only one man, however, is biased:

- **The case of Andy:** Andy works in the oil and gas industry. He is an enthusiastic heterosexual who cannot accept working with gay men. When asked what the problem was, he flushed with emotion and practically sputtered with rage as he said, "Those people are just wrong; I can't stand thinking about the perverted things they do on the weekends. I wish they would just stay away."
- **The case of Thomas:** Thomas is an equally enthusiastic heterosexual who works with the same gay men and does so without complaint. How does he feel about them? When asked he says, "I don't believe in their lifestyle and sure don't understand it, but as long as they do their job, I can't see as it's any of my business." Period. Thomas's reaction was nothing more than a calm statement of a personal opinion about a given way of living.

Thomas felt no anger, no fear, no accompanying flush or sputter, and because there was no emotion, very likely, no bias either. Just because Thomas does not agree with or even like the lifestyle of his colleagues, does not mean he is biased against them. He has the right to his opinion and because of his lack of emotion around the subject is able to keep that opinion from coloring his view of the essential worth of his gay colleagues. Andy, on the other hand, sees the group as so threatening and so flawed that he can't even stand to be around them.

This Exploration Point gives you an opportunity to evaluate the degree of emotion attached to the reactions you came up with in Strategy I.

You may not, in every case, be able to identify a precise emotion. Perhaps, as one contributor said, you "just feel kind of negative." The idea is to see if the thought itself strikes some type of an emotional chord, however faint. If it does, there is a good chance that you have what would be considered a bias against that group.

E *x p l o r a t i o n*
P *o i n t*

1. Pick five kinship groups from the previous list about which you had a significant first thought. Add to the list any other groups about which you have a strong feeling.

2. Beside each category, record any measurable emotion that you experienced when thinking about or encountering that group.

STRATEGY IV: EXAMINE YOUR ATTITUDES TOWARD HUMAN DIFFERENCE

Observing your thoughts and emotions as you think of and encounter other kinship groups is a good start toward bias identification. There is still, however, one more piece of evidence that needs to be collected. To bring charges of bias against ourselves, we need to shore up our case by examining how we feel about the notion of difference itself.

Generally, those who have few biases tend to be fairly indifferent to whether or not a person is diverse.

People who possess the lucrative virtue of seeing others clearly neither ignore the difference nor put excessive emphasis on it. Where do you fit?

When We Notice Differences Too Little

My friend Elise shared with me an incident that would be comical if it weren't such a good example of how not to handle differences. It hap-

pened when a United Parcel Service driver came to the reception desk
at Elise's work with a package for a new employee named John. John,
you'll need to know to understand how silly this story is, was the one
black employee in the department:

> When the driver asked where he could find John, the re-
> ceptionist pointed down the hall to a cluster of men and women
> standing by the copy machine. The driver, never having seen
> the new employee before, inquired, "Which one is John?" Elise
> then watched with amusement as her colleagues spent three
> minutes trying to describe John without mentioning that he was
> black. Impatient, Elise finally, and much to her colleagues' dis-
> may, announced, "John's the black guy over by the window."

There was a time when Jim Adamson, currently chairman of Kmart
and formerly chief executive officer of the parent company of Denny's
Restaurants, would have also been dismayed at Elise's candor. Adamson,
whose tenure at Denny's included the period when they were climbing
out of a morass of discrimination suits, was heard to say, "You know, we
need to be color-blind; we can't see color." Ray Hood Phillips, his Diversity Director, reprimanded him with a gentle, "Jim we do have differences; you need to recognize that." Adamson learned from Phillips's
admonition and claims that one reason the organization made so much
progress in the area of diversity is that it stopped pretending that everyone in the United States was the same.[1]

E *x p l o r a t i o n*
P *o i n t*

Have you ever pretended
not to notice someone's
difference even when it
was pertinent to the situation? If so, what group
or groups were involved?
Were any of these the
same groups against
which you identified a bias
in the previous activities?

Adamson is right, not everyone in the
United States is the same; there is, in fact,
more difference here than in any other nation on earth. And when that difference is
pertinent to the situation, it is perfectly appropriate—and nonbiased—to notice it. In
John's case, the color of his skin was a reality
that needed to be acknowledged to get the
job done (the package delivered). As we'll
see, the fact that John's colleagues were reluctant to mention or (allegedly) even notice
that he was black, is very possibly evidence of
their own biased attitude.

Just as Elise's colleagues' reluctance to
mention John's race does not bode well for
their attitude toward John, our hesitance to

notice a difference when pertinent might be another clue to our biases. This is because:

Denying a difference, when it is pertinent to the situation, suggests that we feel there is something wrong with that difference.

To ignore a disability or skin color or accent or gender is to imply that those differences and our feelings about those differences are so ugly, so dangerous, and so embarrassing, that we had best pretend they do not exist. In other words, the denial of the difference, even to ourselves, can be a way to cover up how we really feel about it. If, for example, we secretly believe that having an accent means the speaker is stupid, what more effective way to keep that bias from showing than to pretend we don't notice the accent at all? If we look down on black people, I can't think of a better strategy for concealing that bias than to create the impression that we are such good people that our saintly eyes don't even glimpse color distinctions much less denigrate them.

In this connection, I am proud to say that I did not deny the differences embodied in the young man who was wheeled into a spot next to me at a recent diversity conference:

There was no ignoring the fact Randy could not use his arms, that his legs were shriveled, and that he would need some help. I'll admit that at first I was a little befuddled. What do I do? Do I do anything? For the fleetest of moments, it crossed my mind to pretend there was no problem, no difference. Fortunately, that moment passed and I knew it was ridiculous to deny that the man had a disability and that he would require some assistance.

Once I made that adjustment, I proceeded to ask Randy matter-of-factly if he wanted me to move over one seat to give him more room. He answered, with no more self-consciousness than if I'd offered him a cup of coffee, that that would be a good idea so he could lay the handout on the seat beside him. Curious, I asked him why he wanted to do that. He answered, again very casually, that with the handout on the chair, he could turn the pages with his feet.

Had I succumbed to the urge to ignore Randy's difference, not only would I have put him at further disadvantage, but I would also have created a distance and self-consciousness between us. His disability is a fact that needed to be acknowledged and accommodated, and accommodation is not bias; it is friendship, and compassion, and human respect.

There are differences between kinship groups and those differences matter. Of course, as we have seen, we can't generalize about an entire population, but on the other hand, neither can we throw out those differences altogether.

> *If a difference is pertinent to a situation, it is our obligation to take it into consideration.*

To do otherwise is to deny an important part of a person's heritage, who they are, and what they have to contribute to our lives.

When We Notice Differences Too Much

Having said all that, it is also a sign of bias when we make too much of a person's kinship group. I wonder, for example, to this day, what the fact that the woman was "Asian looking" had to do with Harold's story about the real estate agent who sold him his new condo. I'm also curious why the loud football players who disrupted my colleague's client dinner at a fancy restaurant had to be described as black. If my colleague were trying to distinguish a particular football player so I would know who he was, that would have been different. In this situation, however, mentioning skin color was as pertinent to the story as the chef's special or the name of the waiter's girlfriend. Perhaps color and all it meant to him were just a little too much on my colleague's mind. This Exploration Point will help you discover if you are afflicted with the same distortion of thinking.

Put down the book and take a minute to think about it. Could the fact you mentioned the identity of the kinship group mean that the person's ethnicity or religion or sexual orientation was too central to your thinking? Is the group you mentioned one of the ones toward whom you had a strong reaction earlier in this chapter? If so, you just might have a bias on your hands.

E x p l o r a t i o n P o i n t

Think of a time when you recounted an incident and mentioned a participant's kinship group in the story. Did that detail really add something the listener needed to know to understand the event? If not, why did you include that information?

CONCLUSION: LOOKING TOWARD THE NEXT STEP

Now that you have discovered your biases—many of which I imagine were quite a surprise—the next step is to figure out the function that each one serves. Yes, biases do have a function, they do benefit us in some ways. In most cases that benefit is temporary at best, but it is a benefit nonetheless. After the benefit is identified, you then will be asked to weigh it against the damage each bias causes. That information will, in turn, enable you to pick the most destructive biases as the ones on which to focus for the balance of the Vision Renewal Process.

CHAPTER SUMMARY

- Many of us are reluctant to admit our biases because we feel that to have a bias means that we no longer are nice people.
- Although biases are not desirable, they are not, unless they are extreme, automatically signs of bad character.
- Behaviors, even if inappropriate, do not necessarily indicate a biased attitude.
- One way to become aware of our biases is to observe the thought that comes to mind in response to a kinship group and gauge how much emotion is attached to it. The more emotion, the more likely the belief is, in fact, a bias.
- Those of us who put either too much or too little emphasis on the ways in which a person is different are more apt to have a bias against that person's kinship group.

4

STEP TWO: IDENTIFY THE ALLEGED BENEFITS OF YOUR BIASES

CHAPTER FOCUS QUESTION

What secondary gains and benefits do I receive from believing in my biases?

In the aftermath of September 11, 2001, Arab-Americans were the unhappy targets of biased people of all stripes. I met one of these unfortunates on September 30 of that fateful year. I don't remember his name, but I do remember his pain and the glimpse I had of the rage that lurked just below his courteous demeanor. He was a Lebanese cabdriver, and he was frustrated and more than a little frightened at how badly some of his passengers had treated him since the World Trade Center attacks.

Most of those who hurt this man so deeply were merely abrupt or cold or sat stiffly in the backseat with frightened looks in their eyes. One woman, however, opened the cab door, took in the driver's Semitic features and Arab accent, and started yelling, "I wouldn't ride with someone like you. Why don't you go home and leave our country alone?" The driver admitted he lost his temper and lobbed obscenities at the back of the would-be passenger as she scurried away in search of a driver with a lighter complexion.

As he told his story, I could tell the man was ashamed of his reaction. It was obvious that those obscenities had sprung from a need to hide the hurt caused by the passenger's refusal to see him for what he was: an immigrant who loved America and had worked hard to make a living in what he firmly believed was the greatest nation on earth.

The passenger had a personal belief, a bias, that was both dangerous and, except for how much it upset everybody in its path, seemingly pointless. It didn't make her any happier and certainly didn't help her form more fulfilling relationships. So why did she persist in believing as she did? The answer lies in the truism of the human mind that all otherwise unproductive attitudes, including biases, carry with them some benefit, some secondary and usually temporary gain. The benefit that our frightened taxi fare got from her bias against Arabs was the illusion that she could predict how they would behave; that illusion, in turn, made her feel marginally more secure in her increasingly insecure world.

This chapter is based on the premise that every bias has some benefit attached to it. Some of those benefits are real for the moment, some are illusions, but, in every case, they are one of the reasons we acquire bias in the first place. Your task in this chapter is to figure out the secondary gains that accompany the biases you identified in Step One. To help you do this, the chapter is divided into several sections, each of which discusses an alleged benefit of having a bias. These include:

- Relief of guilt
- Protection of status
- Protection from loss
- Protection from emotional pain
- Provision of excuses for our behavior
- Protection of community or individual values

BIASES ALLEGEDLY RELIEVE FEELINGS OF GUILT

One often-unrecognized secondary gain from bias is the relief from feelings of guilt. The first-century Roman historian Tacitus was talking about guilt when he said, "It is human nature to hate those we have injured." When we injure someone, we feel guilt. To relieve that guilt, we struggle to justify what we have done. One way to accomplish this questionable goal is to convince ourselves that the person we have injured is in some way inferior and, therefore, deserves our ill-treatment. In short, we make ourselves feel better by becoming biased against them.

Even a historical injury from which we are chronologically removed—American slavery is a good example—can trigger a defensive reaction that causes us to dislike the victim. The demon of defensiveness whispers in our guilty ear, "You don't feel too bad. You don't like 'those people' much anyway. They deserve the way they were

E *x p l o r a t i o n*
P *o i n t*

Do any of the biases you identified in the last chapter carry with them the benefit of relieving guilt? How has this benefit shown itself in your life? Does it really work?

treated." Most people believe in a just world. Surely, we reason, if a group is so downtrodden, they must have done something to deserve their denigration.

BIASES ALLEGEDLY PROTECT US FROM DIMINISHED STATUS

Even the horrific bias that early European settlers had against the native populations of the New World can be explained by a secondary gain. In their case, that gain was the protection of their status as civilized human beings. Isolated, stranded in an unfamiliar environment far from the lace curtains and polished pewter of which they were so fond, the Europeans feared they might slide down a muddy slope and land in a heap beside what they perceived to be the uncivilized inhabitants of "their" new land. To reassure themselves that they were still socially refined, the settlers needed to create a sharp contrast between themselves and their Native American neighbors. They did this by cultivating the illusion that the Native Americans were profoundly and, most telling, "naturally" barbaric. The doctrine of the noble savage aside, this bias served in their minds to utterly distinguish the "them" from the "us" and eliminate any danger of the "civilized" group being mistaken for the "savage."

More than 300 years later, Marie, a Mexican-born nurse practitioner, had a similar concern. She complained of constantly being assigned to care for "those dirty, uneducated Mexican immigrants." As it turns out, her bias came directly from the fear that her contact with these patients would somehow pull her back down into a status and a lifestyle that she

E *x p l o r a t i o n*
P *o i n t*

Do any of the biases you identified in the last chapter carry with them the benefit of helping you feel more certain of your status in society? How has this benefit shown itself in your life? Does it really work?

now finds repulsive. To relieve this fear, Marie manufactured the bias that her former countrymen were irrevocably beneath her in terms of their position in the social strata and, to hear her tell it, in possession of remarkably few redeeming virtues.

One would think that Marie's personal experience with the pain of low status would beget compassion for others. Unfortunately, the opposite is often true. In fact, bias is one way in which we relieve our insecurities by enabling us to look down on others from a precarious perch of imaginary superiority.

BIASES ALLEGEDLY PROTECT US FROM LOSS

Fear of losing something we believe to be rightfully ours is one of the most common reasons for the development of a bias. This explains why biases increase in times of economic slowdown and why it is then that we begin to hear a medley of mantras about how "those people" are "taking all the jobs," "getting preferential treatment," and "taking advantage of the situation." Yale psychologists Carl Hovland and Robert Sears, working in the 1920s and 1930s, found that when cotton prices in the South went down, the number of lynchings increased.[1] Legend or myth or fact—it's hard to tell from this distance—tells us that when the Roman Empire was crumbling, Christians were more frequently fed to lions. True or not, we do know that this penchant for using bias as a way to protect our supply of limited resources has been with humankind since the early days of civilization.

Nan, a bank manager in southern California, provides us with a modern example of how this process works:

> I had worked at the branch for several years and we always had good employees. That is until I hired Akbar, a young man who had immigrated from Iran. At first everything was fine, but then Akbar started acting strangely, staying late, and being generally uncommunicative. One Monday morning, he failed to show up. We soon realized that Akbar was gone, along with thousands of dollars of our customers' deposits.

When my Regional Supervisor found out what happened, he was furious and blamed me for not having made a better hiring decision. It even looked for a while like they were going to fire me. To this day, I have trouble objectively evaluating any Iranian applicant. I'm trying, but I keep thinking they all will be like Akbar and I sure don't want my job to be on the line again.

The truth is that Nan's bias—"All Iranians are thieves"—did temporarily benefit her by making her feel more secure about her job. Ultimately, however, there is a potentially very high price to pay for this ridiculous exercise in inflexible generalities. I realize that the structure of this book calls for me to deal with the price of bias in the next chapter, but Nan's potential price is just too juicy to delay mentioning. If Nan sticks by her bias and continues to refuse to hire Iranian employees, she and her organization are at risk on two fronts. First, and most obviously, they are at risk of being sued for discrimination—and the complaint would be both legally and morally valid. Second, and this is more a certainty than a risk, they will miss out on the many fine employees that no doubt are to be found in the local Iranian community.

E *x p l o r a t i o n*
P *o i n t*

Do any of the biases you identified in the last chapter carry with them the benefit of making you feel protected from loss? How has this benefit shown itself in your life? Does it really work?

BIASES ALLEGEDLY PROTECT US FROM EMOTIONAL PAIN

Mark has a bias. He believes that all fully abled (or, as he is fond of saying with a nod toward Father Time, "temporarily abled") people look down on him and others with disabilities. This misbelief—that all members of a given group are biased—is perhaps the only prejudice that is actually tolerated in the workplace. That toleration is unfortunate because by putting up with the personal fiction that "All men are sexist" or "All white people are racist," or as in Mark's case "All fully abled people look down on people with disabilities," we promote the notion that some biases are acceptable and others are not; nothing could be further from the truth.

Prejudices like Mark's—I'll clumsily call it the *bias bias*—are usually triggered by a desire to protect the misbeliever from a repetition of emotional pain. From Mark's point of view, as destructive as his bias is, it does

E *x p l o r a t i o n*
P *o i n t*

Do any of the biases you
identified in the last
chapter carry with them
the benefit of protecting
you from emotional pain?
How has this benefit
shown itself in your life?
Does it really work?

keep him from being caught off guard next time he is treated like a child or ignored as if he, and his wheelchair, are invisible. Mark, you see, is a paraplegic who for years has been patronized by strangers. Because of these experiences, he has developed a bias against anyone who offers him assistance. The bias is so bad that at even the simplest offer of kindness, he is apt to bristle and snap, "I am perfectly capable of taking care of myself." Sadly, Mark has become just as biased as that minority of people who assume that "All people with disabilities are to be patronized and pitied."

Jesse, a 30-year-old new immigrant from Guatemala, possesses an equally strong desire to protect himself from emotional pain and thus has developed a bias that is as effective as Mark's at shielding him from unexpected blows. Jesse has had a truly rough time of it; he has been laughed at by native-born Americans for his limited English, beaten by a gang of white supremacists, and repeatedly passed over for promotions, all due to his heritage. Because of these experiences, it is understandable—although misguided—that Jesse now holds the bias that "All white people are racist" and sees bigotry everywhere, all the time, in every white person he meets. His own prejudice leads him to interpret the gray areas of each word and action as a sure sign of racism against him and his fellow Latinos. In that sense, his bias has temporarily benefited him by shielding him from any surprises.

BIASES ALLEGEDLY PROVIDE US WITH AN EXCUSE FOR OUR BEHAVIOR

The bias that is the culprit here is our old nemesis and the nice person's bias-of-choice: Guerilla Bias™. As you recall, this brand of bias is based on the premise that emerging group members are in some way fragile; this bias is frequently disguised behind kind thoughts such as "I don't want to hurt their feelings," "I don't want to make anyone upset," or, my personal favorite, "I wouldn't want to risk offending anybody." Because Guerilla Bias is so hard to detect, you would think that its alleged benefit would be equally difficult to determine. In fact, it is really pretty simple:

Guerilla Bias benefits us by providing an excuse to stay away from people around whom we feel uncomfortable.

Here are a few examples of how this thought process plays out to our temporary benefit:

The Waiter and the Wheelchair

- *Behavior:* A waiter ignores the woman with cerebral palsy and asks her younger male companion what she would like to eat.
- *Alleged reason for the behavior:* "This poor woman has enough problems, I don't want to embarrass her by making her talk. I know she has difficulty speaking clearly."
- *Real reason for the behavior:* The waiter is uncomfortable with people with disabilities and is the one who is embarrassed and wants to avoid the conversation. Certainly it is possible that the woman will have difficulty speaking, but it is she and her companion, not a stranger, who should decide how to handle the situation.

The Manager and the Immigrant

- *Behavior:* A manager makes an effort not to sit next to her newly hired Chinese account executive at the company banquet.
- *Alleged reason for the behavior:* "If I sit next to him, I know he will feel obligated to speak with me because I am his boss and he'll be embarrassed because of his accent. It would be kinder not to put him in that position."
- *Real reason for the behavior:* The manager is afraid she won't understand the man; it is she, not the account executive, who is worried about making a bad impression.

The Manager and the Staff

- *Behavior:* A white manager walks into the cafeteria day after day and deliberately avoids sitting at the table where his black employees are congregated.
- *Alleged reason for the behavior:* "I don't sit with the black employees because I know they have their own culture and I don't want to intrude or make them feel self-conscious."
- *Real reason for the behavior:* Again, the manager is the one who is self-conscious. He is self-conscious because bias has lulled him into believing that his black employees are hypersensitive to every slightly misspoken word and could inadvertently be offended at some-

E *x p l o r a t i o n* P *o i n t*

Do any of the biases you identified in the last chapter carry with them the benefit of making you feel better about minimizing your contact with people who are different from yourself? How has this benefit shown itself in your life? Does it really work?

thing he says. It is safer for all concerned, he figures, to just stay away.

There is a chance, of course, that what these contributors fear—embarrassment, misunderstanding, offense—could come to pass, and let's face it, one way to minimize that risk is to avoid contact. The problem, however, as we will see in the next chapter, is that we pay a painfully high price for this tenuous feeling of security.

BIASES ALLEGEDLY PROTECT OUR COMMUNITY AND INDIVIDUAL VALUES

All was fine in Martha's upscale New Jersey neighborhood: The streets were tree-lined, the houses neatly painted, the residents pleasantly liberal, and the school respectably integrated to the tune of two upper-middle-class black families. All was fine, that is, until another black family moved in and then another and then another. Before these nice people knew it, the black student body at the local school had swelled to a dangerous critical mass of 30 percent. "Those people" were still, mind you, quite civilized. Don't get images in your head of drug-crazed kids who refuse to work at McDonald's because they can make more money dealing cocaine. They were gentile sorts; upper-class, educated, well dressed.

Along with this critical mass of blackness came, you guessed it, a fear followed shortly thereafter by an outbreak of bias. There is not much to fear from one lone black child, or two, or three, but, in suburban white-people's imaginations, a great deal to be afraid of when the average neighborhood complexion contains noticeably more pigment. The fear in this case was not of violence or theft, but a more fundamental terror of losing a way of life and a set of values that were treasured and familiar.

The bias that the new arrivals inspired wasn't sharp-edged; no one came right out and said, "These black people are inferior; get them out of here." This misbelief was more amorphous than that, just a vague feeling that something was amiss and that it would just be better if the interlopers found another place to live. It didn't matter, however, that the bias had fuzzy edges, it still benefited the believers in a very important way: The belief that black people did not belong in the neighborhood served as a stanchion around which the group could rally in its defense of the values and way of life it held so dearly. Never mind that no one was really threatening those values, that was the perception, and bias was the reaction.

When people who are different invade our territory (and it doesn't feel much like an invasion until there are enough intruders to actually change things), we begin to fear that the way things have been before and what we believe in may gradually disappear. When immigrants move in, we fear for the survival of our language; when it is white people, we fear for our sense of solidarity; when the invaders are of another gender, we fear for a level of comfort and "way of doing things" that is familiar. No matter what is being invaded and who the invader is, our biases unite us in a way that makes us feel safe.

> **E** *x p l o r a t i o n*
> **P** *o i n t*
>
> Do any of the biases you identified in the last chapter carry with them the benefit of protecting your values from assault and change? How has this benefit shown itself in your life? Does it really work?

CONCLUSION: A CAUTIONARY NOTE

This is the point in the Vision Renewal Process where you just might be tempted to close this book and abruptly terminate your journey toward bias reduction. Why wouldn't you? In the last chapter you were reassured that biases don't make you a bad person; in this one, you were shown that biases do, in fact, offer benefits. Taking all this into consideration, you'd have every right to ask, "Why not wrap it up right here?" The reason to continue with the Process is that the benefits you have identified are temporary at best, while the price, as you will see in Chapter 5, for holding on to your biases is very steep and destructive and, in many cases, very very permanent.

CHAPTER SUMMARY

- Although biases are destructive in our lives and our workplaces, they also benefit us in some ways. Many of these benefits are illusions, others are temporary, but if we are to decide which misbeliefs deserve our most immediate attention, we must balance those benefits against the damage the biases cause.

- Some biases relieve feelings of guilt over how badly we have behaved toward a particular group. They do this by tricking us into believing that the target of the bias has a characteristic that justifies our ill-treatment.
- Some biases give us the illusion that we are, and deserve to be, of higher status than other groups.
- Biases provide us with the temporary benefit of protection from the loss of something we feel is rightfully ours.
- Biases prevent the repetition of emotional pain. This is particularly true of the bias bias, which holds that certain kinship groups are inevitably biased against others.
- Guerilla Bias allows us to feel better about staying away from people around whom we feel uncomfortable.
- Biases provide us with a unifying attitude around which to rally when we feel that outsiders are threatening our values or our way of life.

5

STEP THREE:
PUT YOUR BIASES
THROUGH TRIAGE

Which of my biases should I work on first?

When my daughter was a teenager, I learned one important lesson: Don't sweat the small stuff. So her room was a mess and her hair was green, she was a good kid and that's what mattered. The same principle applies to healing your biases. Some matter, some (almost) don't.

As we saw in the Introduction, everybody has biases—big ones, small ones, destructive ones, (almost) harmless ones. We need to aim our guns at the biases that do the most damage. In short, pick your fights. For example, lighten up about the fact that you tend to think "All professors are absentminded" or "All French people are good cooks." These generalities may not be entirely harmless (nor was my daughter's green hair), but you need to expend your energy where it will accomplish the greatest good.

At the end of the day, the only reason to attack a bias is because it is harmful.

We need to go after those biases that either cause pain or interfere with our ability to function successfully.

In Chapter 3, you identified several biases that are candidates for immediate attention. Just as injured soldiers on the battlefield are put through a triage process to discover who requires treatment first, your biases need to be triaged to identify which ones most urgently require your attention. This is accomplished by balancing the benefits you explored in the last chapter against the damage your bias is apt to cause in the workplace. You will then select the three biases with the poorest ratio of benefit to harm.

To make this triage process easier, this chapter provides six of the most common ways that biases compromise success in the workplace:

1. Biases interfere with hiring the best people.
2. Biases interfere with employee retention.
3. Biases diminish corporate productivity and individual success.
4. Biases interfere with effective teams.
5. Biases compromise sales efforts.
6. Biases result in litigation.

DOES YOUR BIAS COMPROMISE YOUR ABILITY TO HIRE THE BEST PEOPLE?

Linda would have had to answer this question with a regretful "Yes." The Human Resources Director at a prestigious hotel in Beverly Hills, Linda allowed her bias to interfere with a key hiring decision. The mishap occurred during an interview for an important Director of Sales position. Had we been watching the interview through a one-way mirror, we would have seen a look of complete befuddlement on Linda's face. Despite her extensive professional experience, she found herself in a quandary:

> Sitting across the desk from Linda was an applicant who, by anyone's standards, was perfect for the job: outgoing, articulate, and very knowledgeable of the hospitality industry. She was also born and raised in Japan. Therein lay Linda's problem. Because of Mariko's heritage, Linda's evaluation of her was grossly distorted by another set of qualifications, or I should say misqualifications, that popped into her head. All Linda could see as she looked at Mariko was a hodgepodge of stereotypes right out of a Hollywood movie: shy, retiring, soft-spoken, and certainly not good material for a high-stakes sales position.

Linda had a choice to make: Shove her bias and these fictional characteristics aside long enough to see Mariko for who she was and hire her, or rationalize away Mariko's assertiveness so Linda could prove that her bias was correct. Unfortunately for both of them, Linda decided to let her bias rule the day and rule her decision: Mariko did not get the job.

Linda is a classic example of a person who not only has a bias but refuses to let it go even when confronted with external evidence that contradicts what she believes. Linda was desperate to prove herself right. It took a little doing (and, remember, all of this is happening at lightning speed), but Linda was able to rationalize her bias into an apparent reality. She did this by saying to herself that Mariko was just pretending to be assertive because she thought that would get her the job. "In 'real life,'" Linda said to herself, "she must be shy and retiring and soft-spoken."

Linda paid an expensive price for this exercise in belief perseverance. Shortly after the ill-fated interview, Mariko was snapped up by a neighboring hotel, which then, with Mariko's help, absconded with much of Linda's lucrative convention business.

There are other ways that a bias can compromise our ability to hire the right person for the job. Take, for example, what happens with respect to people with disabilities. Legalities aside, if we were really honest, many of us would admit that we tend to define applicants who have physical challenges by one thing only: their disability. If we were wiser, we would realize that no matter how severe the problem, a disability is only one aspect of who the person is and only one small dimension of what she has to offer to the workplace. Following are three examples of just such people. Their names are Barbara Ceconi, Kurt Kuss, and Steve Hanamura and they are, among many other things, blind. I'll admit that when we first met, I did define these three multifaceted human beings as blind and that's OK because, at the beginning, that's pretty much all I knew about them. As I got to know them better, however, their other facets began to emerge and now I think of them as, yes, blind (no miracles have occurred), but also as people with many other dimensions as well:

- *Barbara is many things.* A college graduate, a guide dog owner, a woman, a blonde, a writer, an educator, a professional speaker, a blind person, an elected official, an advocate, a consultant, a daughter, an aunt, a bicyclist, a pianist, a diabetic, a wife, and a white person.

E *x p l o r a t i o n*
P *o i n t*

Have any of the biases you identified in Chapter 3 ever interfered with your ability to make an appropriate hiring decision? What were the details of the situation and what would you do differently now? Might any of your biases create similar problems in the future?

- *Kurt is also multifaceted.* He is a chef, a guide dog owner, a husband, a father, a blind person, a trainer, a college graduate, an ex-husband, a diabetic, a jewelry maker, a man, a professional speaker, a potter, a skier, a parent, a white person, and a consultant.
- *Steve's list is filled with surprises.* He is a consultant, a trainer, a Japanese-American, a man, a father, a blind person, a husband, a runner, a bicyclist, a sports fan, a writer, a singer, a professional speaker, an author, a sports fan (he asked me to mention that twice), a biography buff, a Christian, and a son.

As the labor market goes up and down and spikes and dips and does all manner of things to keep companies and their human resources folks on their toes, one thing remains the same: We need to hire the best person for the job, a task that is impossible if we allow our biases to get in the way. Whether devaluing a person with a disability or cloaking an applicant in imaginary qualifications—good or bad—biases are the enemy that skews our choices, blocks our view, and costs us the talent we so desperately need.

The Exploration Point above is the first of several that you will be asked to complete in your quest to identify the biases that most interfere with your effective functioning in the workplace. It is possible that as you read you will become aware of biases that didn't appear in Chapter 3. If so, just add them to your list and continue to assess their impact as you move through the balance of the chapter.

DOES YOUR BIAS INTERFERE WITH YOUR ABILITY TO RETAIN QUALITY EMPLOYEES?

When Hector walked to the front of the auditorium following my diversity workshop at a California bank, I wasn't much in the mood to talk. It had been a long day and I was anxious to get to my room, order my beloved room service, and see what movies were available on pay-per-view that night. Hector, however, looked anxious to speak his piece so I reluctantly put down my laptop and gave him my full attention. Now I'm glad I did. Here is what he had to say:

> I've worked for this bank ever since I graduated college. I figured I'd be here the rest of my career. That is until the company decided to open locations in the Latino community and transferred me from my old branch on the West side. I was very successful before, but just can't seem to make this new assignment work. I'm thinking of moving to another company where I'd have a better chance to get ahead.

Hector, by the way, was one of five Latino branch managers who approached me with this identical complaint. Each one was promising and bright and each was ready to quit because of the prejudice their managers had against them. The managers' bias went something like this: "All Latinos are familiar with Latino culture, speak Spanish, and would regard it as an honor to work with 'their own.'" Hector, if given the chance, would dispute this generality by saying something like, "There's more to me than having Mexican grandparents, I barely understand much less speak Spanish, and, quite frankly, the culture just doesn't interest me much."

Hector personifies just one way in which bias can interfere with employee retention. Here are three very different but equally wasteful scenarios:

The Case of Angie

- *Background:* Angie, who worked for a graphic design firm, is an exceptionally attractive woman, one of those people who grew up being the reluctant recipient of all those "Gee, you ought to be a model" statements. She was tall, had a great body and beautiful face, and, much to the constant irritation of her female boss, a remarkable ability to look fabulous in inexpensive clothes. There was, however, a problem with those clothes. They were just a little too skimpy and a little too tight, and the colors just a little too loud. None of this was enough to get her reprimanded, but it sure was enough to distort her boss's view of what Angie had to offer the organization. Angie, by the way, was a highly skilled graphic artist.
- *Bias:* Despite external evidence to the contrary (Angie's artwork), Angie's boss could never shake the bias that Angie had gotten her job because of her looks not because of her talent.

- *Damage done:* Angie was deprived of a lucrative promotion. Following that disappointment, she resigned and took a better opportunity with a competing design firm.

The Case of Joe

- *Background:* Joe grew up in a lower-middle-class black community in Washington, D.C. His mother was a schoolteacher and his father a garage mechanic. From the very beginning, Joe showed exceptional intelligence. He attended Harvard University on an affirmative action program and graduated at the top of his class.
- *Bias:* Joe's boss could not get it out of her head that the only reason Joe had succeeded was affirmative action and was, therefore, utterly unable to see Joe's considerable talents for what they were.
- *Damage done:* Because the boss failed to give Joe opportunities for challenge and exposure, Joe eventually felt stifled and quit to take a vice presidency in a parallel industry.

The Case of Esther

- *Background:* Esther had struggled for years to lose weight. Between her metabolism and a back injury that prevented aerobic exercise, she just can't keep it off. Although her weight interfered with a social life in college, she made up for it with intense study and graduated at the top of her business school class.

- *Bias:* Despite all of Esther's achievements, the CEO, who was a physical fitness buff, could not rid himself of the belief that at some level Esther must be lazy and have some psychological "thing" about eating.
- *Damage done:* Because of his bias, Esther's boss gave the vice president's job, for which Esther was next in line, to a less-qualified and less-experienced woman. Esther quit in frustration and eventually began her own firm.

E *x p l o r a t i o n*
P *o i n t*

Have any of the biases you identified in Chapter 3 ever interfered with your ability to retain quality employees? What were the details of the situation and what would you do differently now? Might any of your biases create similar problems in the future?

Hector, Angie, Joe, and Esther—all had top talent and all were lost to their organizations because of bias.

DOES YOUR BIAS INTERFERE WITH CORPORATE PRODUCTIVITY AND INDIVIDUAL SUCCESS?

One of the really creepy things about biases is that they can easily become self-fulfilling prophecies. If a manager believes that an employee has a certain characteristic, darn if she doesn't find a way to make that characteristic come true. The promising black fighter pilots who flunked out of flight school in disproportionate numbers know what I mean. An investigation revealed that some white instructors felt the black pilots lacked the skills to fly safely. As a result of this bias, and in a misguided effort to save themselves and the airplane, the instructors were grabbing the controls prematurely, thus depriving the pilots of the chance to show their capability.[1] These instructors held the bias, "Black pilots can't quite cut it," and found a way to make that bias come true.

Most of us are in no position to grab anyone's controls, but we all have the power to actualize our biases through our failure to coach diverse groups appropriately. This is exactly what happened to a Filipino nurse named Susan whom I met when conducting a needs assessment for a medical center in New Jersey. As Susan stepped tentatively into the tiny room that had been set aside for the meeting, she seemed nervous and ready at any point to flee the interview:

Susan looked at me with complete bewilderment as she struggled to explain why she and the other Filipinos on her floor were performing less well than the non-Filipino nurses. Practically in tears, she said, "Nobody ever tells us what we are doing wrong. I think they think it will hurt our feelings or maybe they just assume we can't get it right. Sometimes it makes me feel like just giving up."

Roger Ackerman, former chairman and CEO of Corning, Inc., would have reacted strongly had he eavesdropped on this conversation. During our interview he said to me, "The root of all evil is bad supervisors who give appraisals without being candid." I

Exploration Point

Have any of the biases you identified in Chapter 3 ever become self-fulfilling prophecies? What were the details of the situation and what would you do differently now? Might any of your biases create similar problems in the future?

would modify his quote just a bit to say, "The root of all evil is biased supervisors who give appraisals without facing their biases." Susan, like millions of other potentially valuable employees, will never be able to move up in the organization and is clearly lost to an industry that is ever-hungry for qualified, dedicated health professionals.

DOES YOUR BIAS INTERFERE WITH YOUR ABILITY TO SUSTAIN HARMONIOUS TEAMS?

The woman who approached me following the workshop was utterly confused about how to handle what seemed to be a straightforward management challenge. Her confusion surprised me because she had appeared so bright and experienced during the program. I was surprised, that is, until I realized that she was allowing her own personal brand of Guerilla Bias cloud her judgment. The conversation went something like this:

> I just don't know what to do. I have several Native American employees who are late to work every day. I know they all have reliable transportation so there's really no reason for them to be so lax. All I can figure out is that it must have to do with their culture so I decided to give them some leeway and let them come in any time up to half an hour after everybody else. Now my problem is that the other employees are complaining and want the same flexibility. In my industry, that just isn't going to work. What do I do now?

My response to this woman was a simple, "Why? Why would you allow the Native Americans to come in late when everybody else isn't granted the same privilege?" Her answer was to repeat the fact that maybe there was a cultural reason why they couldn't grasp the notion of punctuality. After talking with her a while, it became clear that cultural differences were not the problem, her bias was. She was another nice person guilty of the Guerilla Bias that emerging group members have needs so special that they have to be given unique privilege. In this case, that attitude had three negative consequences for her efforts to build harmonious teams:

1. It demeaned the Native Americans by implying that they were not able to measure up to the same standard as their colleagues.

2. It diminished productivity by throwing off the early morning work schedule.
3. It created tension among the team and, according to her, caused the non–Native Americans to look down on their colleagues.

The sad thing about these three losses is that they never would have happened had this manager kept her bias in check and held all her employees to the same strict standard of punctuality.

Having said that, reasonable and respectful accommodation of cultural differences is, of course, a hallmark of a healthy diverse workplace. To help you understand what is reasonable and what is not, here is an example of an adjustment that made sense. It took place at an auto manufacturing plant in Kentucky where employees of various kinship groups complained about the music being played on the manufacturing floor. In an attempt to accommodate everybody's tastes, management decided to pipe in each group's favorite music on one particular day of the week: country on Monday, urban rock on Tuesday, classical on Wednesday, oldies on Thursday, and contemporary rock on Friday. Sure some people still complained, but, by and large, the situation was nicely resolved: no resentment, no bad feelings, and, most important, no increased bias against any one group that had been given preferential treatment.

In my experience, adjustments such as this one rarely create resentment. It is when managers fall into the trap of Guerilla Bias and bend over backward to accommodate any one group that trouble begins and productivity declines.

E *x p l o r a t i o n*
P *o i n t*

Have any of the biases you identified in Chapter 3 ever interfered with your ability to sustain a harmonious team? What were the details of the situation and what would you do differently now? Might any of your biases create similar problems in the future?

DOES YOUR BIAS COMPROMISE THE SUCCESS OF YOUR SALES EFFORTS?

Ted is an elegant man: educated, soft-spoken, obviously intelligent. He is also black. With a trace of irony that he obviously enjoyed, Ted recounted the story of how he went into a Mercedes dealership ready to pay cash for a new car and was ignored. Willing to give the sales staff the benefit of the doubt—it was a busy Sunday after all—he left and came back again: still ignored. That was enough for Ted, he had spent enough years being discriminated against to know when to quit; he took his business elsewhere.

Ted's departure was not, however, the end of the story. Being a man of action with an admitted weakness for genteel revenge, he swung back past the original dealership on his way home from picking up his spanking new S-class sedan. When he told the manager what had happened, she appeared to be genuinely outraged. All the outrage in the world, however, could not reclaim the lost sale of one of the priciest cars on the market.

Ted's story is, of course, the sad result of a kind of bias that has become a cliché: The blatant bias that a black person will not have the resources to pay for a product. There, are, however, an unlimited number of more subtle biases that will also cost you lucrative sales and that make their appearance in a variety of contexts, including:

- Those pertaining to language differences
- Those pertaining to confusion over the identity of the decision maker
- Those pertaining to discretionary income
- Those pertaining to cultural characteristics
- Those pertaining to negotiation strategies

Here are some examples of what can happen when we let our biases come between us and the customer. Do any of them seem familiar?

- **The case of Greta:** Greta, a sales associate for a prestigious line of automobiles, was determined to be fair and to refute the ancient prejudice that men make the family decisions about large purchases. The problem was, she carried her reform too far and now has managed to create a brand new bias: "All woman are the decision makers when it comes to buying a car." Unfortunately for Greta and her sales record, she applied this bias to a couple who came in looking for a late-model previously owned SUV. The bias that seduced her into focusing only on the wife was so robust that it prevented her from seeing the not-too-subtle cues from the woman that the purchase was her husband's decision. When the sales associate persisted in ignoring the husband and following the woman all over the lot, the couple got so irritated that they left and bought the car from another dealership.

- **The case of Coreen:** Coreen is in pharmaceutical sales. She has lots of experience working with foreign-born doctors and does pretty well in that arena. When it comes to physicians from India, however, she can't seem to succeed. She "knows" they are sexist, however, and figures that's the reason she's having so much difficulty selling to them. She also has trouble deciphering their heavy accents and assumes they can't understand what she is saying either. As it turns out, it was Coreen's bias, not the doctors' sexism or English language skills, that was the problem. Because she expected the physicians to treat her badly and not to understand what she was saying, she approached them cautiously, restrained her usual charm and warmth, and cut her visits short. It is no surprise that as the number of Indian physicians increased in her territory, her sales figures declined.

- **The case of Ray:** Corporate real estate has always fascinated Ray. Ever since he paid his way through college working for a local company, he has been good at the ins and outs of the "big deal." In recent years, however, he has been less successful. The variable seems to be that he is working with a larger number of international buyers and is having difficulty making the cultural adjustment. His colleagues eventually noticed that Ray seemed to be approaching all potential clients as if they were "out to get him." Ray later admitted that he had a bias that people from other cultures are dishonest when it came to negotiating business. Rather then assuming the best, like he would for a domestic sale, he went into every deal with his guard up. This is hardly the way to build business.

You may have noticed that Greta, Coreen, and Ray have two things in common. First, of course, they all have a specific bias toward a specific group. Second, and more important, all three have allowed their bias to erase from their memory this most fundamental principle of good sales strategy:

Take time to assess the individual needs of your customer.

E *x p l o r a t i o n*
P *o i n t*

Have any of the biases you identified in Chapter 3 ever interfered with your ability to do business with people different from yourself? What were the details of the situation and what would you do differently now? Might any of your biases create similar problems in the future?

DOES YOUR BIAS PUT YOUR ORGANIZATION AT RISK FOR LITIGATION?

Racist jokes, gay bashing, sexual harassment, litigation: I'll bet I have your attention now. Litigation is the worst nightmare of every organization, every manager, and every CEO. Tragically, this particular nightmare has a way of coming true with alarming regularity. Sometimes the waking dream is filled with contemptible characters who tell racist jokes, denigrate gay people, or make sleazy comments to female subordinates. Other times, and this is the real worry, the act that results in litigation is of the Guerilla Bias variety: no sleazy and easily identifiable characters in sight.

I doubt, for example, that the manager who inspired Meg's discrimination suit was particularly sleazy, he was probably even "nice." Because he was so nice, he couldn't bring himself to tell her that she was doing a bad job; he was, you see, afraid that Meg, who is black, would think he was discriminating against her. Eventually, the manager fired Meg for poor performance. This wouldn't, of course, have been a problem had he given Meg some warning along with the information she needed to improve. Unfortunately, he didn't give her these things; what he did give her were clear grounds for a discrimination suit that, by the way, Meg ultimately won.

Most frontline sales associates and customer contact staff are basically nice people too, but being nice is never a surefire defense against litigation. Here's how one nice person's bias cost her hotel chain thousands of dollars in legal fees:

> It took the man three hours to get drunk and disorderly at the hotel bar, but only a few minutes to turn one small lie into a discrimination suit. Julio was so drunk that it amazed everyone that he was able to find his way to the reception desk and ask for a room, but he did and that's when the trouble began. Realizing she couldn't rent to Julio because of his condition, the clerk pretended to check the computer then turned to him and lied: "I'm sorry, sir, there are no rooms available; I'm afraid I'll have to ask you to leave."
>
> Upon hearing the bad news, Julio uttered a few well-used obscenities and staggered away only to collapse in a nearby chair. Within a few minutes, a white couple approached the desk, asked if there were any vacancies and were handed the key to a room

on the 14th floor. Julio overheard this exchange and, even in his bleary state, understood its significance. Once he sobered up, it didn't take him long to find a lawyer and sue for discrimination.

When later asked why she didn't tell Julio the truth, the clerk said she didn't want him to think she was discriminating against Latinos and said, "If he had been white, I probably would have just told him we don't rent to people who are drunk and sent him on his way." Nobody is saying we ought to call even one rowdy customer a drunk, but in some ways it would have been better, and even oddly more respectful, than treating the man as if he were incapable of handling the truth. The irony is that the clerk's dishonesty created exactly what she was trying to prevent: expensive litigation and more expensive bad publicity.

E *x p l o r a t i o n* **P** *o i n t*

Examine your list of biases to see if any of them has the potential to bring litigation against your organization. Don't just think of the obvious scenario. Use your imagination. How could even the subtlest of prejudices make someone feel that they are treated unfairly or create a hostile work environment?

CONCLUSION: PREPARING FOR THE NEXT STEP

E *x p l o r a t i o n* **P** *o i n t*

After studying the observations you have made while reading the last two chapters, identify the biases that have the poorest ratio of alleged benefit to potential damage. Those are the ones you will work on throughout the rest of the Vision Renewal Process and that will be referred to as your "target biases."

CHAPTER SUMMARY

- The biases that most deserve our attention are those that carry the least desirable balance between alleged benefits and the damage they cause in the workplace.

- Biases interfere with appropriate hiring decisions by negating our ability to evaluate applicants accurately.
- Biases threaten the retention of quality employees in many ways, including when they distort our perception of what individuals of diverse backgrounds have to offer.
- Biases interfere with individual productivity and success by causing us to hold team members to a low standard of performance, preventing us from providing appropriate feedback, and causing us to act on our biases in such a way that they become self-fulfilling prophecies.
- Guerilla Biases interfere with the harmony of diverse teams when they seduce us into giving unreasonable preferential treatment to emerging groups.
- Biases interfere with successful sales when they cause us to misinterpret the buying power, needs, or attitudes of potential customers.
- Bias has a way of resulting in litigation, not only when it is blatant and coarse, but also when it is masquerading as good intentions and seemingly gentle acts.

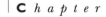

STEP FOUR:
DISSECT YOUR BIASES

How can I test the validity and accuracy of my biases?

Lynn remembers it clearly (sort of). It happened many, many times (but she can't exactly remember when). (Almost) every time she was teamed with one of "them," they were so lazy she had to do all the work (mostly). Besides, she heard from her friend that the ones he worked with were that way, too.

Vague memories, questionable experiences, rumors—not exactly what I would call reliable sources of information. Lynn obviously needs to undergo the next step in the Vision Renewal Process. She, like most of us, must dissect her biases to show how unreliable they are. Although this stage of the process can be fun, especially if you enjoy thinking analytically, it can also be a little embarrassing when we discover the fragile foundation on which most of our biases are built.

There are two parts to Step Four. Both use logic, as Jennifer James puts it, to "move our responses to others out of our guts and into our minds."[1] In the first part ("The Inquisition"), you will be asked three questions, each of which is designed to weaken your faith in your target biases. In the second section ("Glad to Make Your Acquaintance"), you will be invited to gain exposure to people and information that will further erode the premises on which your biases are based.

THE INQUISITION

Question 1: Where did you learn each bias and under what circumstances? For the sake of illustration, let's pick a bias that I held for many years: "Black men whom I don't know are apt to be dangerous in some way." To answer the question of where I learned this prejudice, I have to look at three possible sources:

1. *Parents:* My parents were, as I mentioned earlier, ambivalent racists. As a result of having lived with a mix of experiences and cultural messages, they were left precariously balanced between the mores of 1930s white America and 1960s semienlightenment. They were, therefore, in some ways wise and in other ways ignorant. Unfortunately, just enough 1930s attitude remained in them to negatively influence my thinking.
2. *Media:* There is no need to belabor this point; we all know how much the media enjoys depicting black men as threatening creatures of the night.
3. *Experience:* This is where it gets tricky. We looked at this subject a bit in Chapter 2 ("Carefully Taught: How Bias Is Learned"), but, because experience is such an important part of how we learn our biases, there is more to be said about how this complex and unpredictable process works.

Of all the ways we learn bias, you would think that experience would be the most reliable. After all, we were there, we lived it, we know what happened. Well, maybe and maybe not.

E *x p l o r a t i o n* **P** *o i n t*

Subject each of your target biases to the questions in this section. If possible, answer each question before reading the explanatory material. This may result in getting more accurate answers. If, however, you are confused about what the question means, go ahead and read the illustrations before answering.

We have to remember that any experience with one individual or even ten individuals says nothing about other members of that kinship group. In addition, unless an experience is well rounded and repeated, it tells us little, even about the person we actually encountered. That is because:

The experience may not mean what we think it does.

For one thing, most experiences that give rise to bias are brief and one-dimensional. Each is like a snapshot taken from one angle only and that angle is, by physical necessity, from the perspective of the person holding the camera. The other side of the subject, and the subtleties of shading and dimension that would accurately reflect the subject's appearance, are never recorded. If you don't believe me, think of the number of times you have reacted to a photo of yourself by asking, often with considerable trepidation, "That doesn't look like me, does it?"

Another reason brief encounters are unreliable is that they are distorted by the emotion we bring to them, emotions that mean we can't trust what our senses are telling us. Most of the time, it is OK to trust our senses; if we didn't, we'd be wandering around wasting a lot of energy questioning every sight, sound, and conversation. This trust is what is known as a *zero-order belief*. Zero-order beliefs are those assumptions that are so fundamental to our thought process that we don't even think of them as beliefs. To us they are firm and nonnegotiable absolutes.

Because we trust our senses so profoundly, we forget that factors other than senses affect how we perceive a person or event. Fear, guilt, anxiety, and myriad other emotions, for example, can cause us to think that something happened differently than it did. Emotion, I have to admit, certainly played a role in the experience that contributed to my bias about "dangerous" black men.

The setting for this particularly distorting experience was a gas station in an upscale southern California neighborhood. It being in the dark days before cell phones, I had pulled into the station to make an urgent call at the pay phone. In my rush and knowing I would not be long, I parked in an unmarked spot. Just as I was about to dial the number, a young black man walked up, stood within what felt like six inches of my face, looked me straight in the eye with an intensity I will never forget, and demanded that I move the car.

I know, I know, right about now you're thinking, No wonder she was upset, that's pretty scary. Well, sort of. Yes, my perception at the time was that the attendant was angry and about to lose control. However, when

I look back on the incident now I realize that both the young man and myself would have been better served had I suspended just a bit of zero-order belief in my senses that day. What I haven't told you yet is that I was pretty agitated myself when I pulled into that gas station. There had been a mishap at the university and I was rushing to a colleague's house to see if we could resolve the problem. I suspect that anyone who stood in my way that stressful afternoon would have seemed hostile. It is very possible that my own emotions influenced my evaluation of a young man who was just doing his job. Whether this man was indeed threatening or my senses misled me, I experienced and remembered the incident as negative and frightening.

Family, media, experience—each of these can give rise to bias. This is unfortunate because each also supplies us with notoriously faulty data on which to form an opinion that influences so much of how we view the world.

Question 2: How often have you actually experienced meeting people who conform to your bias? Caution! "Actually experienced" does not include media images or rumor or what other people say they know; all that counts here are personal encounters between yourself and members of the group in question. You will notice that I have deliberately said "encounters" not "encounter." Too often biases grow out of one experience with one person or, at most, with one small group of people.

On top of that, even if a negative situation is encountered repeatedly, the percentage of any kinship group with which you have direct experience will still be absurdly small.

Ask yourself: "How many actual people of this group have I met who have this characteristic?"

For Hannah, that number was three. Hannah bears the burden of believing "All men are sexist." She believes this because she has had three sexists bosses in her 25-year career. Now let's see if we can figure this out. There are 125,000,000 men in the United States. Hannah knows three who are sexist. This means that in her direct experience—which is the only experience she can count on and, as we saw, even that might be faulty—she knows for sure that .000002 percent of American men are sexist. I don't know about you, but I can't even grasp how small a percentage that is. My accountant tells me it is less than two millionths of 1 percent, hardly a statistic on which to base your opinion of an entire population of people.

Judging from the number of antigay jokes Dan tells and how he feels about male homosexuals, you would think he'd had numerous negative encounters with gay men. As it turns out, it was only one and not a particularly disturbing one at that:

> I didn't realize until years later why I felt so threatened by gay men. One day my wife asked me why it was such a big thing to me and I realized it all went back to one incident when I was hitchhiking. The driver made a pass at me. Nothing forced, in fact he was very tentative about it, but it always left me with icky feelings.

I can't say that Dan's bias spontaneously disappeared when he realized it grew out of only one experience, but this revelation did bring his fear into perspective and provided him some leverage with which to reevaluate his attitude.

By the way, I promised earlier that I'd confess how many bad experiences I have had with black men. I also promised that this chapter would embarrass you from time to time. Well, it's my turn to be embarrassed. That number is a whopping, statistically significant, two. Two, and remember one of those men may have just been doing his job.

Question 3: Have you ever met a member of the kinship group against which you have a bias who does NOT conform to your misbelief? I am reminded of Rose who said, "All Mexicans are destructive" (we met her back in Chapter 2). After she told of the two teenagers who tried to invade her home and how that event had spawned her bias, I asked her about the other Mexicans in her neighborhood. She said, without any apparent awareness of the contradiction, that they were all wonderful people. When I pointed out the inconsistency between "All Mexicans are destructive" and "All Mexicans are wonderful people," it was obviously a revelation to her and under the bright light of logic, you could almost see her bias melt away. Sadly, the intensity of her negative experience with the two boys had clouded her memory of the good people around whom she had built her life.

There is, of course, always the off chance that every single one of your encounters with the group toward which you are biased has been bad. If this happens, it doesn't mean your bias is correct, it just means that you must work a little harder to expose yourself to a wider variety of kinship group members.

GLAD TO MAKE YOUR ACQUAINTANCE

Personal Contact

There is a story floating around that may be apocryphal, but like most good fiction, it is well designed to make its point. Supposedly, some children were asked this question: Who is better, the kids in your town or the children in the neighboring village? "The kids in our town" was the speedy reply. When asked why they felt this way, the children answered, "It's because I don't know those other kids." The point of this anecdote is that the more experience we have with a group, the more apt those experiences are to be broad and thus the less apt we are to develop a bias against them.

Another reason that exposure, if it is broad enough and positive enough, diffuses bias is that the more exposure we have to a group, the more knowledge we acquire, and, therefore, the less afraid we will be. Ralph Waldo Emerson said:

"Knowledge is the antidote to fear."[2]

Singer Buchanan, currently EEO Commissioner for the State of Kentucky, provided me with a good example of the importance of acquiring knowledge of other groups. Singer, who is black, was the object of one young white man's fear and bias simply because the man had rarely been around black people. Singer made a special effort to spend time with the man and eventually the fear and the bias were gone. Of course it is not always this simple, but familiarity, if practiced with a truly receptive heart, is far more apt to breed understanding than contempt.

Speaking of familiarity and tight-knit groups, what comes to mind when you think of the following setting?

Night shift at the post office

Is your mind flooded with images of listless low-lifes sleeping on sacks of mail or, in between bouts of fistfights and sleazy flirtations, rifling through envelopes looking for cash and endorsed checks?

I'll admit media images like these got to me too when I was offered the opportunity to conduct a diversity workshop at a local post office in the wee hours of the night. Once I met the trainees, however, I had only one thing to say to the man who hired me: "You don't need me. These folks are doing great." Two Vietnam veterans, a young Filipina, an older Latina, two black men, and an Italian made a wonderful team. The humor they exchanged and the good-hearted connection they obviously shared made me embarrassed that I was standing there supposedly telling them something they didn't know about how to get along. Clearly their time spent in such close proximity, combined with the fact that they shared a common task, had allowed them to work through any problems and get to know each other as people not just as distorted reflections of a painful and divisive past.

Knowledge

Although personal, goal-focused contact like that experienced at the San Diego Post Office is the best way to get to know others and thus reduce biases against them, objective knowledge about various kinship groups can also be helpful. Unfortunately, much of what we think we know about various groups is distorted through the media and exaggerated by rumor and idle conversation. Because of these faulty sources, my guess is that most of you won't do particularly well on the quiz on page 94. The purpose is not to make you feel inadequate, however, but to show how little even the most educated of us knows about other groups and how much we have to learn.

A word of caution before moving to the next step: Do not allow the knowledge gained in this quiz, or any place else for that matter, to congeal into a new bias. Just as information gained through contact with one individual applies only to that person, so, too, knowledge of a group acquired via a statistic applies to the indicated percentage only. Any statistic, no matter how accurately researched, still leaves thousands— or millions—of unique individuals yet to be known and understood.

CHAPTER SUMMARY

- By looking at each of our biases logically, we weaken its power to interfere with our accurate perceptions of others. We can do this in several ways: Question the source of the bias; question the experience that caused the bias; assess how many times we actually have encountered people who conform to the bias along with any experiences with people who do not; and gain more exposure to and knowledge of diverse groups.
- Experiences that spawn biases can be distorted by many things, including the emotions and expectations that we bring to the interaction.

E *x p l o r a t i o n* **P** *o i n t*

1. Describe the average welfare recipient.
2. What percentage of Latinos living in the United States think that new immigrants should learn English?
3. What percentage of women think appearance is a very important consideration when purchasing a car?
4. With which emerging group do white people feel they have the most in common? Black Americans? Asian-Americans? Latinos? People of Arab ancestry?

Let's see how you did:

Question 1: The typical welfare recipient is a white woman living with her two children in a rural area.[3] Most people guess: a single mother, black, living in the inner city with at least three children.

Question 2: A whopping 90 percent of Latinos feel very strongly that U.S. residents should learn English.[4] So much for the bias that immigrants don't feel a responsibility to learn the language of their adopted country.

Question 3: *Woman's Day* magazine found that only 5 percent of women thought looks were very important when buying a car.

Question 4: A study conducted by the National Conference for Community and Justice discovered that most white people feel they have more in common with black Americans than with any group other than their own.[5] This statistic may reflect a certain amount of naïvete on the part of white people, but in view of our divisive history, it is probably good news.

- Most bias-creating encounters are with an extremely small number of kinship group members.
- Increased exposure to a kinship group will decrease our biases against its members if two conditions are in place: that exposure is broad enough and we are able to view the individuals we encounter accurately.

7

STEP FIVE: IDENTIFY
COMMON KINSHIP GROUPS

CHAPTER FOCUS QUESTION

*How can I redefine my kinship groups to minimize my biases against people
I perceive as different from myself?*

Even she was amazed as she watched herself reach out and sweep the contents off the top of the secretary's desk. College-educated, bright, usually reserved, Alice had been hired over the phone for a long-sought-after position. A common tale, you've heard it or lived it before. She showed up at the office only to see the receptionist's face turn white and watch as she scurried away into a nearby office. The receptionist returned a few minutes later accompanied in her wake by the sound of a door slamming and the strains of her boss's voice yelling, "Get her out of here, how could you be so stupid? You know we don't hire colored people."

It was futile for the secretary to make excuses. Alice knew what had happened, it had happened before, and before, and before. She was tired and she lost control. She could no longer restrain her frustration and anger. Now a manager at a large West Coast bank, Alice tells the story without pride but with a certain understandable justification.

Prue, 78 years old and the wife of a retired oil executive, never swept anything off anyone's desk. Maybe it would have done her some good if she had for you can still hear her pain 60 years after the incident. Prue speaks of her lofty professional aspirations when she graduated at the top of her MBA class from the University of Texas. She soon found, however, that despite the temporary progress made by women during World War II, the oil business had no interest in hiring a professional female in 1948. By contrast, her husband, who admits his grades were "Just OK," stepped easily into his first job and rose rapidly in the organization.

Prue has regrets. She doesn't regret the family she raised nor the support she gave her husband through the years; she regrets and grieves over the career that never was. Alice and Prue are different women. One is black, one white, one raised in California, one in Texas, but they share the same frustration, a frustration caused by bias and discrimination. In that sense, they are members of the same kinship group. No longer separated by black and white or age or geography, their shared experience, if recognized, would broaden for each a previously narrow sense of "usness" to include each other.

The next step in the Vision Renewal Process is to do what Alice and Prue might have done: to redefine our kinship groups so that they include those toward whom we hold a bias. This chapter contains five strategies designed to help each of us accomplish this important goal:

1. Acknowledge a shared race.
2. Develop empathy.
3. Identify a shared work ethic and other common values.
4. Identify or create shared goals.
5. Find a shared humanity.

First, however, we'll examine how and why redefining our notion of the group to which we belong automatically diminishes bias.

HOW SHARING A KINSHIP GROUP REDUCES BIAS

As we saw in the Introduction, a kinship group is "any population that shares a self-ascribed or externally ascribed characteristic that sets it apart from others." This characteristic might be a disability, race, gender, age, or any other of dozens of human dimensions. The virtue in the concept of kinship group is that it allows each of us to belong to many groups at once depending on the characteristic on which we focus. It also—and this is the best part—enables us to broaden our group to include many populations that we previously thought of as different from ourselves.

One of the many advantages of sharing a kinship group is that:

Once you identify yourself with a particular population, members of that group are transformed in your mind from "them" to "us."

When this happens, we automatically begin to evaluate members of that group more fairly. This is because human beings have a tendency to give their own "kind" a break. When members of the group with which we identify do something bad, we figure it is because of circumstances; if they do something good, it is because of character. When, on the other hand, people from another group do something bad, it is because of character; if they do something good, it is because of circumstances.[1]

This dubious reasoning created problems at a bank in New York City where the Vietnamese-born manager complained that her Puerto Rican tellers didn't grasp the procedures as fast as the Vietnamese members of the team. "I suppose it's just that they have a different attitude toward learning [*character*]," she said. When asked if she ever had any Vietnamese who learned slowly, she admitted that she had. She was then asked why she thought that was true. Her explanation is a classic example of how we give our own kinship group the benefit of the doubt:

> Well, it's really different with the Vietnamese. It's not that they don't want to learn; it's just that they live in such close quarters with their large families that they don't always get enough sleep. Sometimes they come to work so tired they can't think. They even make mistakes from time to time, but, under those conditions, who can blame them [*circumstance*]?

E *x p l o r a t i o n* **P** *o i n t*

How might this manager's attitude toward the differences between Vietnamese and Puerto Rican employees interfere with her ability to manage effectively?

She said nothing about a differing attitude toward learning or any other character trait.

Scholars dating back to the time of Ruth Benedict would have loved to get a crack at this question. This is because the subject of balancing human difference and human commonality fascinated them. Benedict and her colleagues, in fact, produced extensive research supporting the value of looking beyond cultural boundaries to see what we share with other groups. One important study found, for example, that people are quicker to pair positive adjectives with the word *we*, than with *they*.[2] What these findings tell us is:

> The more "we" we can muster, the more commonness we can find between ourselves and other kinship groups, the more positive we will feel about them.

As physicists would say, we must find the wormholes in space, the tiny tubelike connections that allow links to be recognized from far-flung parts of the universe, and, for our purposes here, from seemingly very different "theys."

ACKNOWLEDGE A SHARED "RACE"

As a symbol and reminder of how groundless all this separation is and how easy it should be to identify shared kinship groups, let's pick apart the myth of race and ask the question: How did this notion of racial *we-ness* and *theyness* get started anyway? According to Margaret Mead, it was the boats that messed us up. If only we had spent thousands of years walking from Africa around the world, Meade laments, the gradation in skin color would be so gradual and so slight that no one could possibly start all this silly business about race.[3] But the boat did get invented and the myth of race that anthropologist Ashley Montagu, in *Man's Most Dangerous Myth: The Fallacy of Race*, called "the witchcraft of our time" got invented along with it. Even though there are more genetic differences within so-called racial groups than between them, we still choose to use this imagined thing called race as an excuse for bias and myriad other ills.

Originally concocted by scientists in the 18th century to sort out the occupants of an increasingly complex and far-flung world, race has little to do with physiology. Instead, it is a cultural construct whose roots lie in sociological complexities well beyond the parameters of this book. What we do need to recognize here, however, is that even though racial distinctions are an illusion, the belief that race is real is not and it is that belief that has created all the fuss.

It doesn't take a background in physical anthropology to grasp the frailty of the notion of race. There are notable physical commonalities spread across the globe, across cultures, and across alleged racial lines that immediately expose the lie in this concept. My Swedish husband, for example, has a rare type of arthritis. Who does it hit most often? Northern Swedes and Native American Indians—go figure! Biologist Jared Diamond of University of California at Los Angeles reports that Asians, Native Americans, and Swedes share a scooped-out shape to the back of their front teeth but their immediate neighbors do not. In Africa, most groups are lactose-intolerant except those lucky Fulani in northern Nigeria who, like the Norwegians, can eat as much ice cream as they like.[4]

In fact, the only way we have been able to divide humans into three (or, in the early days, 30) races is to select an arbitrary few characteristics on which to base the classification. If, for example, we lumped people by those who lack the gene that protects them from malaria, then the Xhosa people in southern Africa and the Norwegians are one race. Complexion for sure doesn't do the job, mostly because skin color categories don't correspond with the dozens of other physical characteristics that make us human beings.[5] Speaking of skin, if we go strictly by that, you would think that the sub-Saharan Africans would be closely related racewise to the Australian Aborigines. The fact is they have less in common genetically than any other two groups on earth.[6]

If you still need convincing that racial distinctions are nonsense, try this one: 85 percent of genetic differences between people is not between races or ethnic groups but between individuals within those groups.[7] This means that members of two racial groups can be more alike than members of the same group.[8] *Newsweek* reported, for example, that if any two black people are picked at random and their 23 pairs of chromosomes examined, their genes would probably have less in common than the genes of one of them and the genes of a randomly selected white person.[9]

All this science aside, the absurdity of race is best summed up in a Jim Crow–era saying:

"If a black man wants to sit at the front of the bus, he just puts on a turban."

Colin Powell came right up against the folly of racial categories when scouring the Georgia countryside in search of a meal. When Powell pulled up to the window of a local drive-in, the young woman in attendance said she was from New Jersey and didn't "understand any of this," but that she wasn't allowed to serve him unless he could prove that he was a student from Africa. Apparently, if he had been able to haul out his student visa rather than his Army ID, his so-called race would no longer have mattered. As it was, the woman refused to serve him and Powell had to endure the bias-laden stares of the diners as he sped away in an uncharacteristic display of rage.[10] Powell's humiliation, disturbing as it was to him, was a small one compared to the millions of greater tragedies that have happened all because the culture felt a need to manufacture the myth of racial distinctions.

Having said all this, I wouldn't expect anyone to instantly abandon racial kinship groups with their rich heritage of culture and history. I would, however, invite you to contemplate what it means to be artificially divided by the vagaries of historical trends and the pseudoscience that those trends produced.

ACKNOWLEDGE SHARED EMOTION

Acting coach Constantin Stanislavsky and Sigmund Freud shared the same rough category of race, but they also had something more real in common: both men were preoccupied with the notion of empathy. Freud, when talking about empathy, used the word *einfuhlen,* which means to "find one's way into another's state of mind," or as some have translated it, the "feeling in" process. Stanislavsky's version of "feeling in" and empathy was an acting technique he called the "Magic If" by which actors better understood and got under the skin of their characters.

Actors who use Stanislavsky's technique ask themselves how they would act "if" they had their character's life experience. The odds that an actor would have actually lived the life of Willy Loman or Stanley Kowalski, for example, are so remote that the only way for him to answer that question is to identify experiences of his own that approximate those of the character. The Magic If thus allows one human being to engage emotionally with the experience of another; the Magic If is empathy.

Empathy is putting yourself as best you can inside the other person's perspective and temporarily abandoning your own.

For purposes of our current task of identifying common kinship groups, the empathy we are seeking is summarized in these two questions:

1. If you define yourself as a member of what is considered the majority population, can you empathize with the emotions of those who have traditionally been targets of bias in our culture?

2. If you do not define yourself as a member of the majority population, can you empathize with emotions that the majority might experience that are similar to your own?

These two questions illustrate one of the main points of this book and one of the key things we need to know about reducing bias:

Empathy is a two-way proposition.

This means that we all have an obligation to do the best we can to understand each other's feelings and experiences.

No matter which perspective you hold, the Magic If is key to achieving this kind of understanding. For those of you who question the possibility of achieving empathy between kinship groups who possess substantially different amounts of power and who have been subjected to substantially different intensities of bias, I sympathize with your skepticism. Full understanding of another's life experience is illusive if, as my father used to say, you haven't "been there." Even if you have been there, it is you that was there, not the other person. Everyone's psychological terrain is different. Because of this, the fallout from a given experience will settle on each of us in a unique pattern—deeper here, just a dusting over there. For one person, the fallout may not stick at all, for someone else, it may pile so high that it suffocates any chance of happiness.

Because of all this, the lucky thing is:

Full understanding is not a prerequisite to empathy.

What we are after—and what we can realistically expect—is a reasonably well-considered grasp of the essence of what the other person is feeling. Take labor pains, for example. "You'd have to experience it to understand" is what my mother used to say about giving birth. It was as if one needed to be a member of an exclusive club to comprehend that particularly eloquent "discomfort" (as they called it in natural childbirth classes—hah!). I'd agree with mother on this one; if you've never had a baby, you'll never know the full depth of the "discomfort." At the same time, it is still possible to "get it" enough to meet the needs of a woman in labor and to have an intelligent conversation about what she is going through.

To notch the pain down a peg or two (and broaden the metaphor to both genders), let's talk about headaches. Everybody's head hurts at one time or another. Some endure the steady drone of a tension headache, while others feel a burning sensation in their sinuses; for the most afflicted, their curse is the blinding constriction of a migraine. Having been blessed by the gods, I have never had a migraine headache; I have, however, had my share of tension. Because I haven't "been there" with the pain of dilating capillaries, I am incapable of fully grasping my assistant's agony when demon migraine comes to call. I have tasted her discomfort through my tension headaches though and, with a little imagination, can transport myself into a "virtual being there" and achieve what philosopher George Harris calls a state of sympathetic emotional engagement.[11] Likewise, the able-bodied person who is temporarily disabled by a broken leg will never feel the same amount of frustration experienced by a person permanently confined to a wheelchair. But, she can approximate his emotion and thus feel enough empathy to form with this man, and with others like him, a new kinship group. This particular group would be composed of members who understand to varying degrees what it feels like to be limited by a disability.

Although the techniques of the Magic If can be used to form kinship groups around any emotion, our priority is to see how much empathy we can muster for the experiences of those we think of as most different from ourselves. In particular, we strive to share an understanding of what it is like to be the target of a bias.

Like headaches, the pain caused by bias comes in several flavors. For the quadriplegic, the pain might be the humiliation of being patronized by an ignorant public. Other times, the flavor is grief, fear, or anger. Each of these emotions can be manifested anywhere on a continuum from slight to severe—from mildly spicy to red hot. Here are some examples of this continuum:

- Mild embarrassment to humiliation
- Irritation to rage
- Feeling socially out-of-place to completely excluded
- Being mildly offended to deeply hurt
- Mild anxiety to terror
- Discouragement to hopelessness
- Mild confusion to utter disorientation

It doesn't matter where on that continuum the emotion we have experienced falls, what matters is that we have tasted that particular flavor.

This section consists of stories of people of diverse backgrounds who have experienced, at some point on the continuum, a shared experience related to bias. As you read over the stories, you are encouraged to play the Magic If game, to watch for a spark of recognition, a moment of familiarity, a pang of memory of a time when you felt a similar emotion or found yourself in a similar position. Remember, the degree does not have to be the same, the nature of the discomfort does. Here are some brief examples just to help you better understand the process:

> A woman is angry and frustrated when someone falsely accuses her of homophobia.
> *Because of those emotions, she is able to* . . . approximate the pain of and empathize with the fear and frustration of a male friend falsely accused of sexism.
> A black person is hurt and angry when accused of a crime merely because of the color of his skin.
> *Because of that emotion, he is able to* . . . understand the pain of the white woman who is unfairly charged with racism.
> A white Christian is hurt when he overhears a colleague make a snide remark about his religion.
> *Because of that emotion, he is able to* . . . sympathize with a Muslim colleague who finds an anti-Muslim joke taped to his locker at work.

Identity Confusion

Question: Have you ever felt unsure of your identity, of which kinship group you belong to, or of the role you are supposed to play? If so, then you can probably "If" your way to feeling empathy and an expanded sense of kinship for the characters in this section. From a Filipino immigrant to a middle-class white male to a Japanese-American who cannot see, their stories have a great deal in common:

- **The case of Greg:** The year was 1963 and Greg had just arrived in this country. We find him standing outside a pair of "colored" and "whites only" bathrooms in Mississippi gazing down at the brown skin on his arm wondering which bathroom to use.
- **The case of Henry:** Henry, a white native-born American, is confused too, but his identity confusion is not confined to one humiliating moment. It is with him every day as he struggles to decipher the changing rules of the game that no longer make his role clear in the community and the workplace. From whether or not to open a door for a woman to the perceived threat of affirmative action,

Henry, who used to be so confident, doesn't know who he is anymore.

- **The case of Steve:** My friend and colleague Steve Hanamura tells his story: "As a child I and all the other kids at the blind school wanted nothing more than to be like other children. Through the years, we experimented with lots of ways to achieve this unlikely goal. One time, for example, a friend and I decided to pretend that we could see. We were determined to venture out alone—just the two of us—and walk down the street in such a way that no one could guess that we weren't sighted. To achieve this impression, it was important that we not hold on to each other.

  "I shudder now to think how we looked. The strategy was to walk with arms at our sides (like we imagined sighted people to do) and maintain our sense of direction by occasionally brushing arms as we moved. This may have fooled the people walking past us, but it didn't do us much good when it came to navigating safely around the obstacles that sighted people take for granted. My friend, clinging to an ice-cream cone, fell straight down an open utility hole. When he pulled himself out, uninjured and unbowed, the only thing that bothered him was that he had lost his cone!"

E *x p l o r a t i o n*
P *o i n t*

Have you ever had an experience that would help you relate to what Greg, Henry, and Steve felt? Can you, despite your background, use the Magic If to empathize with a Filipino immigrant, a white male, and, as he calls himself, "a blind Japanese guy"? Think about the details of the moment and how it made you feel.

Greg and Henry and Steve have all experienced identity confusion and the accompanying muddle over how to behave. Are these emotions at the same point on the continuum of severity? Do their experiences taste equally bitter? Certainly not. No matter how confused Henry, or any other white male, may feel, he always has the comfort of knowing that the culture as a whole embraces him. This disclaimer aside, Henry can still use his own emotion as a reference point for understanding and empathizing with Greg and Steve. Greg and Steve, likewise, can use their knowledge of Henry's experience to better understand how much they share. See the Exploration Point at left.

If you were able to recall an experience and empathize with those who have been in this position, you are well on your way to globalizing your kinship.

Minority for a Moment

Question: Have you ever felt like a minority? This might mean to feel excluded, ignored, embarrassed, disadvantaged, and/or dozens of other emotions. The following are the stories of three women who have experienced at least some of these uncomfortable feelings:

- **The case of Mai:** Mai struggled gamely to keep her eyes from filling with tears as she recounted how hard it was for her to move up in the organization. Although she was basically good at her job, she just didn't have the English language skills that would allow her to form the kind of contacts that are necessary for advancement.
- **The case of Elena:** Without a trace of self-pity, Elena recounted how she was ignored when trying to make a purchase at a department store. Apparently the clerk felt that the elegantly dressed English-speaking customer standing behind Elena was more worthy of her attention than the Mexican immigrant who didn't appear to speak much English. The clerk's bias was clear when she deliberately reached past Elena to take the other woman's purchase.
- **The case of Kim:** Kim, a young lawyer at a prestigious male-dominated law firm, was unable to learn about important firm policies because she was excluded from the chronically all-male lunches. It is not that her colleagues were being deliberately discriminatory, they were merely indulging their natural urge to relax with people whom they perceived to be most like themselves, in this case, other men. Regardless of her colleagues' motivation, Kim still was deprived of the valuable information she needed to succeed.

Can any of you who are not members of an emerging group look within your own experience to see if you have ever been in a similar position or felt a similar emotion?

To make it easier for you to answer this question and possibly jog your memory and "Ifing" skills, here are stories of four men who have far more in common with Mai, Elena, and Kim than you might initially think:

- **The case of Roger:** Working on the floor of a primarily male manufacturing plant, Roger found himself perched precariously atop an ideological soapbox one hot afternoon defending three women who claimed that the sexual jokes told by their male colleagues amounted to sexual harassment. Although Roger's colleagues didn't blatantly call him gay, the message was clear in the audible titters, smiles, and winks of his male teammates.

- **The case of Jeff:** When Jeff, a white police officer, stopped a black student outside the local high school for a traffic violation, he was immediately met with a collective chant of "Pigs, Pigs, Pigs." Upon being handed the citation to sign, the young man pulled a tissue from his pocket and used it to hold the officer's pen; he didn't want his skin to come in contact with an object that an LAPD cop had touched. After hastily scribbling his signature, the youth made an elaborate show of throwing the pen on the ground.

- **The case of Tom:** Tom tells his story: I had just graduated college in Theater Arts when I heard of an opening in an executive training program at a local studio. I sent my résumé and followed up with a phone call. It was easy to get the human resources manager on the phone because, as he told me, I was perfect for the job. With a new baby and rent in short supply, I was very excited; at last, I thought, all that hard work has paid off. Then the bombshell came. "I have to ask you one thing," he said, "What is your race?" When I heard the question, my bubble burst and, judging from his tone of voice, so did his. He said, "If you had been black or Hispanic, I'd hire you right this minute, but because you are white, I can't even consider your qualifications."

- **The case of Rick:** Rick is a white male who had always been able to build professional contacts easily. That is until he went to work for a Chinese-owned company. Initially Rick was optimistic about his future there, but became discouraged when his usual charm and glibness went unappreciated. The problem? Culture and language differences were getting in his way.

Roger, Jeff, Tom, and Rick were able to get over their discomfort. After all, they had the entire culture to fall back on. That does not mean, however, that these men didn't learn something important from their pain: how to empathize with those who don't, unfortunately, share their mantle of white privilege.

Anyone can be made to feel like a minority. This bitter status is not the sole property of gay people, women, people with disabilities, or any emerging group. Everyone has felt the sting of exclusion. Perhaps the dart lodges deeper in the hearts of the less powerful, but it is unjust to assume that men and the majority have never approximated that pain;

E *x p l o r a t i o n* **P** *o i n t*

Whether you are a member of the so-called majority or of an emerging group, use the appropriate stories in this section to help you empathize with people different from yourself. Recall a time when you felt excluded or on the short end because of the kinship group you belong to.

- If you are of the majority, what do your own emotions tell you about how members of emerging groups might feel? How would your experience differ from theirs? Does your increased understanding weaken any of your biases?

- If you are from an emerging group, are you surprised to learn that majority populations have experienced discomfort as well? How might that realization impact the biases that you have chosen to work on?

and that is good news. It is good news because we can use that common discomfort to begin, as 1990s jargon would have it, to "get it." That process of getting it is one way in which we can broaden our definition of the groups with which we identify and the people we think of as "us."

Lost in the Language

Om någon av er är av svensk börd kan ni förstå denna paragraf. För den som inte är svensk kan denna paragraf lära er att färstå, hur det känus att vara förvirrad. Dessa ord har översatts av min tillgivne svärfar dr Åke Sandler, som jag kommer att nämna i nästa kapitel. Fastän jag har stor tilltro till Åkes förmåg med översättningen, är det ändock nedstämmande, att ha ett avsnitt i min bok jag själv inte kan läsa. I det avseendet tjänar dette exampel som bevis på, hur det känns att förlora kontrollen.[12]

No, you're not hallucinating. The previous paragraph was in a language other than English. In fact, it was Swedish (it is translated in the endnote). It felt pretty weird coming across it all of a sudden, didn't it? That moment of disorientation will help you understand what Mai feels as she struggles to decipher the subtle jokes of her colleagues. Next time you become impatient with a nonnative English speaker who looks at you blankly or nods and smiles while pretending to understand only to go ahead and perform a task incorrectly, perhaps you'll have just a little better idea of what a strain it is to communicate across the barrier of language.

Being Devalued

Question: Have your achievements ever been devalued because of
a perceived advantage? Angie's have. You remember her, she's the exceptionally beautiful woman we met back in Chapter 5 ("Put Your Biases
through Triage"), the one who quit her job because her superiors thought
that all she had to offer were her good looks. Angie's talent was devalued because of one characteristic. Perhaps that has happened to you.

It certainly happened to Lucas. Lucas, in fact, had no problem empathizing with Angie even though it is hard to imagine any two people
more different from each other. Angie is female; Lucas is male. Angie is
28; Lucas is 50. Angie is white and grew up in suburban Illinois; Lucas is
black and was reared in a housing project in Queens. Finally, Angie is
gorgeous and even Lucas would admit that no one could ever say that
his looks were much of an advantage. Despite these differences, Angie
and Lucas have a life experience and an emotion in common: Angie is
sick to death of everyone thinking she got where she is because of her
looks; Lucas is bone-tired of people assuming he achieved his position
because of affirmative action.

Frank, too, is able to empathize with Angie. Frank, whose core kinship group might be defined as "privileged white male," had his own set
of advantages that led people to devalue what he had achieved:

> I'll admit it, in a lot of ways I've had it great: I'm a white
> male; my parents had money; my mother was there every day
> after school; I went to the best schools; I was even a first-string
> football player in college. I really do appreciate all that, but I
> hate it when people act as if I've had happiness handed me on
> a silver platter just because I'm a rich white guy. The other day,
> in fact, some of my colleagues at work came right out and told
> me how easy I've had it compared to them. Well, that might
> be true, but what they don't know and never will is that I've also
> had things to overcome. Mine was an alcoholic father who,
> despite his financial success, vented his frustrations by regularly
> hitting my mother and myself. I don't like talking about it much,
> but my life hasn't been as easy as people think.

Frank has never been belittled because of his looks or because of an
alleged affirmative action advantage, but his efforts have been negated
nonetheless. In his case, everyone believes that Frank got where he is
solely or mostly because of his privileged upbringing. When Frank heard

the stories of Angie and Lucas, there was a wince of recognition on his face and, with that recognition, the hope that he would be able to re-draw the lines of his kinship group to include others whose efforts, like his, have been devalued because of one perceived advantage.

Perhaps some of you might be able to do the same.

LOOK FOR A SHARED WORK ETHIC

As important as it is, empathy and the Magic If is only one way in which we can identify a shared kinship group. Another is to look for values on which we can agree and that, therefore, can become the defining features of new and shared kinship groups. The point in this chapter is not to delineate all the values that can be shared—those are for you to discover. What I want to accomplish here is to illustrate one value that if identified and voiced, can create a shared identity around a common point of view. Because this book is about the workplace, I have chosen to focus on what is commonly referred to as the *work ethic*.

This section is designed to remind us that a work ethic, like so many potentially unifying values, is by no means the exclusive monopoly of native-born Americans; it is a value and, therefore, a kinship group category, that we all can share. None of my contributors said it or lived it better than Zhao Lin Chen. Mr. Chen came to America a scant two years before submitting this item. A retired scientist, he was willing to take what he describes as a "little job" to make a contribution to his adopted country. He painstakingly wrote out his story with a charming mix of pride and humility:

> I have a little job—crossing guard for an elementary school. It is easy to do. But I am very happy doing it. I came to the school in the early morning every day. I stood by the construction area out door, and looked at the traffic, get way for the students. Even if it is snowing or raining, I have to stay there. The people who was going and coming say hello to me. They said great while I stood on the ice in cold winter to work. Some of them gave me something for getting hot. Some time they teach me to speak English.
>
> I met another crossing guard. When we were meeting for the first time. We just said who are you. It is difficult to exchange. But now we become a good friend. We talk about China, America, live, work, history and current, etc. He spoke slowly, and cor-

rected by saying. I taught him to speak some Chinese. I don't have a care. He drove me to be home while it is snowing. When the weather was bad, he told me don't to ride bicycle to work. Even he pick me up to school. The weather was very cold, but my feeling was very warm. He is interesting in Chinese food. I cooked some for him to taste. I have been knew some people who was working on the construction area. They are warm for me. Some one taught me to speak native English. Example: "Hi, brother. What's happening" I love them and my job.

Mr. Chen's story, told with such broken eloquence, puts the lie to the image of the immigrant who comes to America for a free ride and a welfare check. So, too, does the tale of the immigrant women who inhabited the tenements of Manhattan's Lower East Side during the early part of the 20th century. These women valued hard work so highly that they competed to see who would be the first to hang their laundry out on Monday morning; those fluttering shirttails became proud pennants of achievement and colorful testimony to a highly developed work ethic.

Elena's "pennants of achievement" are the cloths she uses to clean the houses of her grateful clients. Elena is just one example of the millions of new Americans with whom we all share a continuing tradition of hard work. During the interview for this book and in those bits of conversation that happen spontaneously as she works around me in my home office, I have learned a lot about Elena—how she married late because she had to care for her mother and how she resents the illegal Mexicans who take welfare and, therefore, have more money than she does. Even though she craves some of their small luxuries, she thinks that what they are doing is wrong. "I was one of them [illegal] once," she admits, "and I never took anything from this great country." The kinship group composed of people like Elena and Mr. Chen and millions of others whose work ethic is central to their lives is one, I'm sure, we are all glad to share.

CREATE A SHARED GOAL

Have you ever been stuck in an elevator? (This one scares me as much as public speaking scares you.) I wager that when this happened, you and your fellow prisoners abandoned all pretense of conventional elevator etiquette: You no longer stood erect, stared forward, looked neither to the left nor right, and, certainly, no longer pretended that you were alone. Also, once the reality set in that the elevator was malfunctioning, any fine distinctions about who belonged to what demographic category instantly dissolved; you were now all members of a newly created kinship group. This particular kinship group was composed of people who had in common the stark terror of being trapped in a small space, being out of control, and possessing no knowledge of when or how the adventure would end. The group also had a shared goal: Get out of there and the sooner the better.

Of course a kinship group born of a temporary experience like being trapped in an elevator has a short life span, but the principle of sharing a common goal applies equally to more lasting aspects of living. Alice, the one who made such a mess of that secretary's desk earlier in this chapter, understood this. Alice, by the way, ended up getting a job and eventually recovered from the pain of being treated so badly by that racist executive. Unfortunately, however, the only difference between her new job and the one she didn't get because of racism was that the second company felt obligated to hire her. Her new white officemates were standoffish at best and she could still feel racism in the air. Alice, and this won't surprise you knowing what we do about this woman, wasn't willing to accept working in an atmosphere of dissension. She set out to fix the situation and did so by figuring out a way to bring the group together behind a common project.

Although Alice didn't realize it at the time, she was creating a new kinship group. Her idea was simple: approach her colleagues about designing ways to improve the functioning of the department. Fortunately, they agreed and a new kinship group was born, a group whose members now shared something that had previously been missing: a specific and measurable goal. Although the creation of a shared goal was not enough to instantly dissolve the racism in the hearts of Alice's colleagues, their common effort did provide a medium of familiarity, and familiarity, as we have seen, is an important first step to reducing any type of bias.

Shared goals have the power to fill the fissure that separates us into kinship groups. When we are striving to achieve the same thing, it is just plain harder to hate each other. Roger Ackerman, formerly of Corning, knows this. Roger grew up in the 1950s and played every sport you could name. His enthusiasm for athletics taught him a fundamental truth that has as much to do with bias as it does with sports: "When in the heat of

E *x p l o r a t i o n*
P *o i n t*

What strategies might you adopt in your workplace to create a new kinship group around shared goals?

battle, it doesn't matter what you are." Another corporate leader, Jim Adamson, had the same experience when first entering a black high school. Jim, who is white, had trouble fitting in until he and his fellow students picked up a basketball and headed for the court. Once he became a really good player, any concern that his black teammates had about the color of Jim's skin melted in the heat of their enthusiasm for winning the game.

IDENTIFY A SHARED HUMANITY

In recent years, I undertook a task that has taught me more about the humanity we share than any other experience of my life. I have begun raising puppies for an organization called Canine Companions for Independence; one of these dogs, a black Labrador named Jazz, is warming my toes as I type these words. The idea is that we raise and train the puppy, give it back for advanced training, and then, if all goes well, eventually have the honor of seeing it placed as an assistance dog to a person with a disability.

This process of raising a puppy is obviously filled with rich emotional experiences, many of which are found in connection with the diversity of people that the dog attracts. For example, as I walk into a restaurant or through a mall or into a movie theater with a puppy named Bliss—a yellow Labrador–Golden Retriever mix festooned in her blue and yellow CCI cape—people of all descriptions approach me to ask about the dog or to beg the favor of a short session of ear scratching (the dog's, not the person's). It is because of these puppies that I have had lengthy conversations with college professors, immigrants, and homeless people, all of whom are drawn to either the love of dogs or the notion of helping someone with a disability. Whether it is the dog or the disability, it is the human connection, the shared kinship group, that counts.

It was also common humanity, in this case combined with the unifying power of music, that turned the awkwardness of a multicultural wedding into a true celebration:

If you had stuck your head in the door of the dimly lit and eerily smoky Chinese restaurant in East San Diego, you would have had trouble making out the colorful scene within. When your eyes finally adjusted to the haze, you would have seen dozens of Vietnamese and Spanish immigrants as well as white native-born Americans standing awkwardly around the room in self-conscious demographically correct pods of like ethnicity. These clusters were the natural outgrowth of the discomfort that accompanies different languages, traditions, and dress. The self-imposed segregation was soon to change, however, and it was the music that, in the end, brought everyone together.

The first entertainment of the evening was in the form of a karaoke song sung by a young man who was the Vietnamese bride's cousin. The song was Frank Sinatra's "My Way" and the man who sang it spoke only Vietnamese and yet he sang quite beautifully in perfect English with hardly a trace of an accent. He seemed instinctively to understand the underlying message—a message that is so American—of individual choice and moral courage.

"My Way" cracked the cultural ice, but it was the flamenco music that brought everyone to their feet, moving at first cautiously away from their respective groups and gradually convening at the edge of the dance floor. Within moments the children were dancing a not-too-bad imitation of the fluid flamenco dancer and the Americans were laughing and applauding and swaying back and forth while rubbing shoulders with traditionally dressed Vietnamese, and even, in the enthusiasm of the moment, giving a smile to a stranger who just months before had been crossing pirate-infested waters or languishing in a refugee camp with little food, fading hopes, and very little music.

Harriet's unifying event was far less pleasant than a wedding, it was a skiing accident. If you had met Harriet's workmates, you would assume they had no problem forming a kinship group. They were all engineers and had plenty of opportunities to get to know each other through shared projects and common goals. In Harriet's case, however, a common occupation and common goals just weren't enough. The problem—or I should say, the perceived problem—was that Harriet was blind and her colleagues could see and somehow they just couldn't quite bridge that gap. That is, until Harriet, very much to the surprise of her sports-loving colleagues, went skiing and broke her leg. As soon as she returned to work, things were different. No longer was the workgroup divided into the categories of "blind person" and "sighted person," they were, instead, united into a newly discovered kinship group, one that values athletics and courage and a willingness to take physical risks for the sake of a good time. No one, her colleagues are fond of saying with a smile, is better at that than Harriet.

E *xploration*
P *oint*

Now you try it. Take a minute to list all the kinship groups to which you belong. (Hopefully, this will take a lot longer than a minute.) These might be based on ethnicity, occupation, shared experiences, shared tastes and interests, shared values, shared goals, or any other category.

If you are a Latino female, you obviously wrote woman and Latina. You might also have said that you were a member of your church. Voilà, your kinship group just expanded by several hundred. Perhaps you are a member of Rotary International. That just bought you, at last count, 1.2 million new kinship group members with whom you can identify. If you said you are a parent, you now magically have a "like me" that includes people of every ethnic group, both genders, many people with disabilities, and, of course, a wide range of ages and religions. The list is infinite and so too are the ways to cut the kinship pie—the ultimate slice being, of course, a kinship group called the human race.

CHAPTER SUMMARY

- One way to diminish bias is to broaden and multiply the number of kinship groups to which we feel we belong. In this way, we create "in-group" connections to people whom we previously thought of as very different from ourselves and thus minimize our biases against them.
- We can expand our notion of racial kinship groups by recognizing that, although a very real societal construct, the notion of race has no physiological foundation.
- One key strategy for identifying common kinship groups is to empathize with the emotions and experiences of those who are otherwise very different from ourselves. This common feeling, even if it is to a different degree, automatically creates a connection that reduces our biases.
- Most populations in the workplace already share a kinship group defined by the value of hard work. This is a connection, and a kinship group, that can be particularly valuable when seeking to build diverse work teams.
- The creation or recognition of common goals is another way in which kinship groups can be created, defined, and unified.
- Every human being is a member of dozens of kinship groups. By shifting focus from one category to another, we discover there are very few people with whom we cannot find something in common.

STEP SIX: SHOVE
YOUR BIASES ASIDE

CHAPTER FOCUS QUESTION

*How can I move my biases out of the way so they no longer
block and distort my view?*

Some years ago, I was strolling
down a street in Los Angeles—nice part of town, broad daylight,
lots of people around. I was also, and this is an important detail,
a perfectly safe distance from the curb. As I walked, a car pulled
up beside me, slowed down, and stopped. Just as I turned to
look at the car, the driver lowered his head so I could see his
face. The moment I saw that his skin was black, I jumped back.
I then had one of those uncomfortable moments that make life
so interesting when the man said, with great dignity and compassion, "That's OK, I understand." He then asked for directions
and continued on his way.

Because this incident took place many years ago, long before I began
my own journey through the Vision Renewal Process, I'll give myself a
break for reacting so defensively to the color of the driver's skin. The
question still remains, however, "Would I jump again today?" The truth?
I honestly don't know. My guess is I would have the urge to jump, but that
my mindfulness, the same mindfulness I am asking from each of you,

would empower me to shove the bias "all black men are dangerous" out of my mind long enough to see the driver for who he most likely is: a man without a map.

It is this shoving aside of our biases that the first five VRP steps were designed to make possible:

- Steps One, Two, and Three made us mindful of what we were fighting and showed us where to focus our energies.
- Step Four ("Dissect Your Bias") showed us the weak foundation on which our biases are built.
- Step Five ("Identify Common Kinship Groups") helped us broaden the groups with which we identify so that we might judge others less harshly.

Now it's time to reap the benefit of all this hard work. Essentially what these first steps did was transform each target bias from a vital force with the power to distort our perceptions into an inert object that can now be picked up and moved anytime it gets in our way. Our biases have, in short, been objectified and converted into nothing more threatening than an irritating habit of thought.

You may have noticed that this is a short chapter. That is because there isn't much to say about Step Six.

Think the thought, shove it aside; think the thought, shove it aside; think the thought, shove it aside.

Simple.

As we have seen, a bias is an attitude and every attitude is at some point manifested as a thought. Often that thought triggers a behavior. Because Jill was such a hard case, I'm going to use her as an example. Jill had what seemed to be an unshakable bias against people over 50. Here's how that bias/thought/behavior progression played out in her case:

- *Underlying bias:* All people over 50 are uncreative and stuck in the past.
- *Thought:* "There is no point in giving Lance that assignment, he'll never come up with the innovation we need."
- *Behavior:* Refusal to give Lance any challenging projects.
- *Consequence:* Lance quits the organization because of lack of opportunity and takes his 25 years of experience elsewhere.

Remember, Jill has already gone through the first five steps so now has the power to stop this train wreck and keep Lance from leaving. The point where Jill needs to throw the switch is just after the thought, "There is no point in giving Lance that assignment" comes into her head. The trick to doing this for Jill, and for us, is to stay in the moment so that we can catch the thought as it whizzes by. This takes practice and vigilance, but it can be done. Also, it helps to realize this important principle:

Shoving a thought out of your mind is a mechanical act.

We are not our thoughts, our thoughts are tools that we produce to help us survive. Because we produced them, we naturally have the power to manipulate them. Again:

Think the thought, shove it aside; think the thought, shove it aside; think the thought, shove it aside.

Even if we can only keep the biased thought out of the way for a few seconds, we can peer through that break in the fog and see the person accurately. Perhaps the fog will close again, but it is a start and, like any mechanical act, shoving the thought aside becomes easier with practice.

The benefits of shoving a bias aside go far beyond the ability to see one individual on one occasion clearly. For one thing, the more we do it, the easier it gets, and eventually manipulating our biases becomes a habit of which we are barely aware. Also, bias-free vision has a cumulative effect. Because it allows us to see people clearly, we suddenly find ourselves meeting more and more individuals who do not conform to our bias. At first, this reality tempts us to think that "they" have changed, evolved, and, in some ways, gotten better; in fact, it is we who have evolved, it is we who have, in many ways, gotten better. As experiences of seeing people accurately accumulate, the balance between past biases and real life begins to tip in favor of accuracy, the bias begins to fade, and, ultimately, cases of mistaken identity become rare occurrences that surprise us rather than daily events of which we are not-so-blissfully unaware.

CHAPTER SUMMARY

- Once we have laid the proper foundation, shoving our biases aside becomes a mechanical act of habit and will.

- The more we practice pushing our biases out of the way, the easier it becomes until, eventually, we do it automatically.
- Seeing people clearly has a cumulative effect. The more we are able to see people as individuals without the intervening distortion of our bias, the more evidence we will have that our bias is wrong.

9

STEP SEVEN: BEWARE
THE BIAS REVIVAL

CHAPTER FOCUS QUESTION

*What do I do if my biased attitude returns and how can I
keep that from happening?*

"When I turned again, Sher-
lock Holmes was standing smiling at me across my study table. I
rose to my feet, stared at him for some seconds in utter amaze-
ment, and then fainted for the first and last time in my life."
—Dr. Watson (via Arthur Conan Doyle, *The Adventure of the
Empty House*)

Literature is filled with unexpected reappearances, some of them
welcome, some terrifying. This quote, of course, refers to one of the
good kinds: Sherlock Holmes's return from his alleged demise at the
hands of the infamous Professor Moriarty. Dr. Watson is surprised, but
he is glad to see his old friend. When your biases return—and they will—
you, like Watson, will be surprised, but you will also wish they had remained a very distant memory.

Biases, like all unhealthy attitudes, have a perverse way of lying in
wait for opportunities to reexert their influence on our lives. One way to
prevent this is to understand the dynamics that allow them to return. In
the case of Sherlock Holmes, he returned because he called upon his

esoteric knowledge of Japanese wrestling to defeat Moriarty and live to tell the tale. The reasons for the reappearance of bias are a bit more complicated.

THE RELUCTANT PATIENT

The primary reason biases return is that we don't really want them to go in the first place. Like a child who wants to stay home from school for just one more day, there are lots of reasons why we might not want to recover from our bias. Maybe we don't want to betray or question the parents who planted the bias in the first place, perhaps we cling to the misbelief because it is like an old shoe that has molded itself into the shape of our thinking and is just too comfortable to take off. Most of all, we resist recovery because we are all a little bit in love with our biases. Biases are our buddies. As we saw in Chapter 4, bias like most bad habits, has its perks. When we drink too much, we feel high. Chocolate tastes good. Smoking calms us down. When we give up those bad habits, let's be honest, we lose something. With bias, we lose, or think we lose, lots of things. Most of all, when we let go of a bias, we lose a false sense of security and enter the frightening and ambiguous world of the real. We are forced to break out of a cocoon of bigotry that is warm and safe (and stifling and stuffy) and enter a more open place where we risk an unpleasant sensation of vulnerability.

I met a young woman some months ago who was saddled with a particularly tenacious infatuation with her biases. I'll call her Pam. Pam was a colorful character, pretty and tough and a heck of a horseback rider. Her skill in riding is no surprise for she had been with the circus since her early teens and traveled the country experiencing adventures so colorful that I'm not sure I wanted to know the details. She did tell me, however, that some of those adventures were the result of biases launched against her from the front porches of small town after small town where her affiliation with the circus was to others sure proof of her ignorance, vulgarity, and, at the very least, questionable morals. None of which, by the way, appeared to be true in her case.

I met Pam when I hired her to guide my daughter and me on a horseback ride near the Mexican border. After a trot on the beach, we headed back to the stables through the low brush. As we maneuvered the trails, Pam pointed repeatedly to the places where illegal aliens would camp. At one point, she spotted a family huddled in the chaparral struggling not to be seen by the Border Patrol officers watching from the hill above. When Pam saw the patrol car, her biases bubbled up as if they had been trapped inside for decades. According to Pam, the Border Patrol officers, each and every one of them if you took her word for it, were mean-spirited, cruel, chauvinistic, and without a trace of human compassion for these immigrants who just wanted to build a better life for their families. Clearly Pam knew what it was like to have bias directed at her and yet she had no awareness that she was generalizing about these officers just as her small-town nemeses had generalized about her.

Riding through the sagebrush on a mesa at the Mexican border was hardly the time to force, ask, or even suggest that Pam examine why she clung so tenaciously to her bias. If I were to guess, however, the answer would involve a secondary gain that was not discussed in Chapter 4, but that is not uncommon. Pam probably clung to her bias against law enforcement because this attitude had come to be part of her identity. Were she to give it up, she would have to abandon a position that helped define her as a person living on the periphery of society, always on guard, and always a bit of a rebel. Abandoning her bias would cost her a sense of self that she desperately needed in her particularly uncertain world. Were Pam to work through the VRP and gain the power to shove her bias against law enforcement aside, it would be her desire for this secondary gain that would put her in jeopardy of a relapse.

INDIVIDUAL ENCOUNTERS AND RESUSCITATING EVENTS

Biases come back to life, not only because we crave the benefits that we think they bring, but because of events that spark their revival. These resuscitating events fall into two categories:

1. Encounters with individuals who conform to the content of our bias
2. External events involving the objects of our bias

Individuals Who Conform to Our Biases

Nothing can resurrect a bias faster than encountering several people who actually conform to what we believe. This happens because biases come from somewhere; someone at some time must have had the characteristics that we turn into biases or this whole bias business never would have began in the first place. When you find yourself confronted with someone who confirms your bias and you can hear your old nemesis knocking at the door, try this:

1. Remind yourself that any one encounter or incident applies only to the specific individuals involved.
2. Go back through other experiences with the group in question and see how many people you have encountered who do not conform to your bias. If you have been exposing yourself sufficiently to members of the group and forcing yourself to see them the way they really are, you will no doubt find plenty of examples that you can use to drive the bias back out the door.
3. Return to Steps Four and Five and run the bias through the secondary gain identification and dissection processes one more time. A refresher course can't hurt, and having been through it before, at this stage of the game, you'll be pleased at how easy it is.

Resuscitating Events

A dramatic event involving the objects of our misbeliefs can be so vivid that it shines a dark light on the soil of our subconscious, warming it just enough to bring to life the dormant seed of bias. Up it pops, just a sprig, but sufficiently healthy to start us once again down the road to destructive habits of thought. The attack, for example, on the World Trade Center on September 11, 2001, caused a renewal of bias against Muslims and Arabs. Bias renewing events do not, however, need to be as grandiose as the bombing of a symbol of Western power. Riots, a murder, employee layoffs, a publicized sexual harassment suit, or a case of violence in the workplace can unlock dormant fears. Once that fear is set free, there is the danger of it being directed, not at the actual perpetrators of the crime, but at those around us who resemble the players in that event; a bias is reborn.

The way to counter the effect of such an occurrence is to undertake a deliberate, immediate, and systematic examination of the event. This inquiry is ultimately about answering one question: *What do you REALLY know about what happened?*

To get that answer, more specific questions must be asked. What these questions are depends, of course, on the nature of the event, but these examples will give you some direction:

If the event resuscitates the inflexible generality that all members of a particular group are biased:

- Did you actually hear the person say a racist comment or was it reported secondhand?
- Did you hear the statement in context or was it an isolated sound bite?

If the event resuscitates a bias that certain groups are violent:

- Has the perpetrator been proven guilty or is guilt just alleged?
- Do you really know the kinship group of the alleged perpetrator or is that just a rumor?
- How many people were involved in the incident?

If the event resuscitates a belief that certain groups get preferential treatment:

- Do you really know that the woman got the promotion because of her gender?
- Do you know the whole truth about why the Latinos were allowed to leave work early or did you just hear one side of the story?

As manager, it is your job not only to watch for your own recurrences of bias but to bring reason and rationality to the workplace on the occasion of a resuscitating event. In the tragic case of an outbreak of war, a class-action suit, or any other happening that might renew bias, you must see to it that rumors are researched, facts corrected, and the event brought into perspective.

FAKE IT TILL YOU MAKE IT

Sometimes, let's face it, a bias can be so deeply rooted, so firmly attached, that we just can't get rid of it, or every time we think it's gone, it comes wandering back like an unwanted houseguest. In that unlikely event, there is still hope:

Act as if you don't have the bias.

Aristotle was a fan of this approach. He knew that attitude follows behavior and with respect to bias he would no doubt have supported the modern dictum: Fake it till you make it.

Psychologist Daryl Bem put it another way: "Saying and doing becomes believing."[1] The psychological truism that underpins this statement is that most of us can't stand doing something that does not conform to what we really feel. This disconnect between action and feeling is called *cognitive dissonance*. Because cognitive dissonance is so unpleasant, something has to give, and if we're stuck with the behavior, we are forced by our discomfort to change our attitude.

The impact of cognitive dissonance is supported by a good deal of research, including one Yale study in which students were paid various amounts of money to write an essay taking a position they did not hold. Those who were paid the least ended up changing their view to conform to what they wrote in the essay; those who were paid the most had a higher toleration for the inconsistency and continued to sustain a position that was different than what they had written. See the Exploration Point below.

The answer to this question is that the extra money allowed the better paid students to more easily justify their deception. They had, after all, been given a substantial amount to act in a way that was dissonant with their beliefs, that is, write an essay with which they did not agree. "A reasonable person," they might conclude, "would betray their values for this much compensation." The money, in essence, bought them out of the discomfort caused by the lack of congruity between belief and action. The poorly paid students lacked the luxury of this excuse. The only way they could continue to feel like honest people was to change their attitude and, thereby, undo the deception.[2] With respect to bias, if we act as if we like a kinship group—act in a way different from our attitude— the discomfort caused by the incongruity might just force us to change how we feel.

<table>
<tr><td>

E x p l o r a t i o n
P o i n t

Why do you think the poorly paid students changed their attitudes while the better compensated ones stuck to their original opinion?

</td><td>

One way to act differently from how we feel, to "fake it," is to use respectful language even when we are not feeling particularly respectful. Jennifer James talks about how saying something out loud, even if we don't believe it, can actually move us closer to holding a view that conforms to what we have said.[3] If this is true, and I believe it is, then speaking negatively of a kinship group and using disrespectful language cannot be a good thing. On the other hand, if we curb negative lan-

</td></tr>
</table>

guage and instead speak positively and respectfully of others, those positive attitudes might just begin to seep into our minds and change how we feel. I am not, by the way, speaking here of externally imposed rules of political correctness. What I am suggesting is that we adopt a personally correct pattern of behavior that not only benefits others but helps us move slowly but surely toward a more enlightened attitude.

Let me create a composite character named Bess to show how beneficial faking it can be. Ever since she can remember, Bess has had, as she put it, a "thing" about people who don't express themselves well. Whether it is that English is their second language or that they lack education, as soon as she hears them speak, her mind is filled with judgments like "unintelligent," "will never be able to do the job" (even if the job has little to do with communication skills), "uncreative," negative etc., negative etc., negative etc.

For whatever reason, Bess just couldn't exterminate this bias. She was aware it existed and aware it distorted her view of many employees who had much to offer the organization, but she still found herself avoiding people who did not articulate up to her standard. The problem became so bad that one staff member, a Latino immigrant, went to Bess and said that he felt she was discriminating against him. Fortunately, they were able to work together to avoid any legal action, but the incident was, for a while, very disruptive to the diverse work team that Bess's manager was trying so hard to develop.

Fictional Bess felt awful about this incident; after all, remember, she is one of the nice people. Determined to change her behavior, Bess made a list of the things her bias was causing her to do and the consequences of those behaviors:

- *Behavior:* Failure to initiate conversations.
  Negative consequences: Perception of discrimination. Alienation of the team.
- *Behavior:* Failure to assign employees to plum projects.
  Negative consequences: Employees' inability to gain valuable experience and exposure. Perception of discrimination.
- *Behavior:* Failure to call on particular team members during meetings.
  Negative consequences: Missed opportunities to voice ideas or ask questions. Perception of discrimination.

Having made her behaviors concrete and measurable, Bess set out to do things differently:

- *Substitute behavior:* Bess consciously began to initiate conversations with people whom she used to ignore.
  Positive consequences: She discovered how much these people had to offer and began to treat them more fairly.
- *Substitute behavior:* Bess started deliberately assigning those employees who were qualified to good projects. Notice, I said, "those who were qualified"; she resisted the temptation to substitute her own bias for a Guerilla Bias in which she patronized someone just because they were different.
  Positive consequences: Most of the employees excelled.
- *Substitute behavior:* Bess began to call on people more equally during meetings and, most important, really listened to what they had to say.
  Positive consequences: She and her team were exposed to different perspectives. Also, the employees were able to gradually hone their communication skills.

The ultimate consequence was that Bess's bias began to fade. It faded because it couldn't survive the onslaught of positive and varied information that Bess' new behaviors caused to come her way. The better she treated people, the better they responded; the better they responded, the more positive her experience; the more positive her experience, the better she felt about a group whom she had previously dismissed. In Bess's case, each positive experience served as a layer of poultice on her festering bias and before she knew it, the wound had healed. Fake it till you make it; it works. See the Exploration Point below.

PASS THE BUCK

One of the promises I made to myself when I started writing this book was to be realistic about bias. One of those realities is that at times you cannot succeed. Shards of past experience and tightly packed layers of fear combine to create a mass just too dense to dislodge. In cases like this, it is time to pass the buck. Rebecca, for example, admits that her eye still catches a glimmer of her childhood bias from time to time.

Rebecca grew up, she recounts, in an environment so thick with bias against black people that it took her years to emerge from

E *x p l o r a t i o n*
P *o i n t*

What other behaviors might you adopt in the workplace to fake an attitude of acceptance and respect?

its influence and, she says reluctantly, "I'm still not quite there." Rebecca knows that if even one tiny fragment of her bias breaks off and floats to the surface, it could distort her ability to make appropriate management decisions. This is a risk Rebecca flat-out refuses to take. As a precaution, she is careful to always have other team members involved when interviewing black candidates and if that isn't enough, she will step aside and let someone else make the decision. Better safe, she figures, than sorry when the equitable treatment of human beings is at stake.

CHAPTER SUMMARY

- One way to minimize the return of biases is to understand why we are reluctant to let them go in the first place. This means to identify the benefits, as we did in Chapter 4, that we feel they bring into our lives.
- Biases can reappear when we encounter people who conform to the belief. When this happens, we need to remind ourselves that the characteristics of any one person are not necessarily typical of the entire group and that if our experience has been broad enough, we have had numerous encounters with individuals who do not share those traits.
- Biases can also reappear in response to dramatic public or workplace events like terrorist attacks or discrimination suits. It is the manager's job to make certain that these events are accurately and thoroughly portrayed.
- Because attitudes have a tendency to mimic behavior, biases that are difficult to dismiss can be weakened by behaving as if they don't exist: fake it till you make it.
- In the face of particularly stubborn biases, it may be necessary to dismiss oneself from decisions involving members of the target kinship group.

GATEWAY EVENTS:

*Entering into
Diversity Dialogue*

No one would say it was a pleasant conversation and no one would dare claim that it didn't take courage to make it happen. It was the mid-1960s and Tony was the only black student at the college. A whiz in chemistry, he sat in class week after week—alone. Six empty seats surrounded him in all directions, that is, until the day Dennis came and sat down beside him, stuck out his hand, and said hello. Dennis was white, and he was tired of submitting to the peer pressure that dictated he avoid Tony—that's the same Tony Polk we met in the Introduction, now Chief Diversity Officer of the American Red Cross.

Dennis and Tony began to talk and Dennis asked some awkward questions: "Why do you want to be with whites anyway? After all, we don't exactly make you feel welcome." "Why aren't most black people very smart?" "Why?" "Why?" "Why?" If there had been a politically correct dictatorship back then, Dennis would have been in trouble, but there wasn't. Dennis took a chance and Dennis got lucky. Tony had the courage to listen and the wisdom to respond.

Tony and Dennis were willing to risk loss of face, anger, even humiliation to have a conversation. Also, they were unwilling to tolerate what Bruce Jacobs in his book *Race Manners* calls a "sterile, exaggerated, civility."[1] You know the kind of thing I mean: The kind of civility that a middle-aged black man described to me as the climate of his all-but-him white neighborhood in Virginia. Nice people, no cross-burning, no name-calling, but little else going on either and, most certainly, no progress being made toward the relief of bias. Jacobs argues that, if we are to make that progress, we need to begin to talk. In the following passage, he speaks of racial differences, but his words apply just as eloquently to any type of diversity and any type of bias:

> From what I have seen of racial card-folding among folks who ought to be arguing, the most dangerous racial assumption is that a black or white acquaintance "won't be able to handle" disagreement or challenge. Please. While zealots are out bombing buildings and burning churches, the rest of us are afraid to talk because we might upset one another? I say let's talk while we can.[2]

Dennis and Tony were willing to talk while they could. They are brave men and Part Three argues that we must follow in their footsteps. We must begin carrying on conversations about bias because conversation is our most powerful weapon against the fear and misunderstanding that surround us; it is also the most powerful tool we have for fighting bias. It is time we risk hurt feelings, discomfort, and even anger. Like that black man in the "civil" white neighborhood said to me, "At some point we have to trust that we have something reasonable to say and take a risk." There is a crisis in courage when it comes to bias and we need to wake up to the fact that diversity is a contact sport. Psychic bruises and a bump or two are always possible, but there is virtue in that conflict if it moves us closer to the goal of clearing our vision and seeing people for who they are.

Fortunately, or unfortunately depending on how you look at it, we rarely have to seek out opportunities to engage in conversations about bias; life has a way of presenting them to us. These opportunities come in the form of misunderstandings, accusations, and any other happening that involves discord between or about people who are different from each other. Because these incidents are capable of bringing about productive dialogue and serve as gateways to greater understanding and reduced bias, I call them *gateway events*. Gateway events appear in many guises. These are just a few:

- Perhaps you witness an act of bias against a friend, acquaintance, or colleague or hear an inappropriate joke or comment.
- Maybe someone falsely accuses you of bias.
- Perhaps someone treats you in a way that appears to reflect a biased attitude.
- Perhaps you say or do something that inadvertently offends someone.
- Maybe you witness someone else being falsely accused of bias.
- Perhaps you are confused and uncomfortable because of the differences between yourself and someone else.
- Perhaps you say or do something involving diversity that you immediately regret.

Regardless of the nature of the gateway event, talking about sticky diversity issues is not always comfortable and not every conversation ends up with the participants collapsing into each others arms in a mutual paroxysm of newfound understanding. The purpose of Part Three is to provide the tools and skills to minimize the discomfort and maximize the chance that we will, if not collapse into each other's arms, at least be able to walk through those gateways and meet on the other side. Believe me, it is worth the effort.

10

THE BENEFITS OF DIVERSITY DIALOGUE

CHAPTER FOCUS QUESTION

How does talking about diversity help reduce bias?

When in recent memory has dialogue about bias been given a better forum than during the O.J. Simpson trial and when in recent memory has an opportunity so brimming with potential been ignored? As it turned out, the trial and its atmosphere were more stifling to conversation than even the most virulent forms of political correctness. The O.J. trial invaded neighborhoods and workplaces like the proverbial elephant. This particular elephant stood swaying in the middle of thousands of dining and meeting rooms, but no one, despite the permeating stench, would acknowledge that the beast was there. Every sound bite, every video clip, offered another opportunity to talk; but rather than seize the day, we ducked the subject and forfeited the benefits of a dialogue that might have transformed a tragic event into a catalyst for healing.

A few weeks after what has ominously come to be called The Verdict, I was sitting at lunch with some black and some white colleagues. The conversation was moving along well—open, lighthearted, interesting—when its path was blocked by that swaying pachyderm and all talk came to an abrupt halt. Someone had brought up the subject of the trial. It took an instant. I could practically hear minds and hearts slamming shut. Body language changed. Oh-so-subtly blacks turned toward blacks, whites toward whites; like turtles we drew back into our respective shells for protection from the discomfort. And none of us did anything about it. No one, not me, not my colleagues, had the courage to acknowledge the creature that had come into our midst. Each of us had an obligation to keep the dialogue going and none of us did a thing about it. Unforgivable.

Had we talked, we might have learned a host of things. Perhaps we would have gained mutual understanding of each other's opinions about law enforcement. Maybe we would have learned that the others at the table weren't a monolithic entity with one view and one set of opinions. Possibly we would have gained a better grasp of each other's life experiences, personal challenges, and views of the world.

The O.J. trial was a gateway event writ large. Like all such happenings, it generated energy. Had we had the wisdom to talk about it more— not among our in group but with so-called outsiders—that conversation would have served as a psychological and social transducer to transform the energy into something positive and enlightening: that conversation would have reduced our biases.

The purpose of this chapter is to examine why conversation like the one we failed to have around the O.J. Simpson trial is such a powerful weapon against bias. The chapter covers three areas:

1. How conversation reduces bias by increasing knowledge and mutual understanding
2. How conversation reduces bias by minimizing and clarifying destructive rumors and misinformation
3. How conversation stifles the spread of bias

BENEFIT: INCREASED KNOWLEDGE AND UNDERSTANDING

Here are the stories of two very different women. One was willing to risk diffusing a bias and thus succeeded in moving the cause of diversity forward. The other allowed her fear of confrontation to seduce her into passing up an opportunity for understanding that would probably never come again.

The woman who was willing to walk bravely through her own personal gateway event was Deborah, a restaurateur in San Diego, California:

Some years ago, I had an unfortunate relationship with a food-and-beverage manager to whom I reported. After being on the job for only a few weeks, he upped my hours, increased my workload, and began to make comments under his breath like "Female executive chef . . . what a joke!" To make matters worse, he was uncomfortable with the fact that I was gay. He even told a coworker that he was determined to "drive out the female chef." I tried to talk to him, to get a good relationship going, but he just wouldn't listen. The final blow came during a management meeting when he and I had a heated difference of opinion. At one point, he was holding a belt that someone had borrowed and returned to him. He slapped his hand with it several times, and said, in front of everyone, that after the meeting he would "teach me a lesson."

As it turns out, I ended up quitting. During my final weeks on the job, I deliberately asked him to attend a local restaurant function with me. During this event, he became aware of my stature in the business community as well as my strong connection with the media and other chefs. After this, he tried everything to get me to stay, even apologizing for his behavior, explaining that in his country women were third-class citizens and that homosexuals were still publicly stoned. Though it was too little too late for me, I found it encouraging that he hired another woman to replace me and he seems to have worked out some of his problems.

Had Deborah not tried to educate this man, he might never have seen the error of his ways. Not only did her successor benefit from Deborah's courage, but so did the entire San Diego restaurant community.

The other woman, the one who backed away from her gateway, was me:

The scene of my cowardice was the dining room of a Los Angeles restaurant where I sat facing a young Harvard graduate. This was no ordinary Ivy League scholar but a young Latino who had managed through sheer grit and intelligence to pull himself out of the ganglands of East Los Angeles. This book was the catalyst for the lunch and my intent was to learn as much as possible about what promised to be a unique perspective on diversity and bias. As it turned out, I learned more about myself than I did about him.

For one thing, I began stereotyping this fellow before I'd even laid eyes on him. As I drove to the lunch, my head was filled with images—and biases—of a brave young man of superior intelligence, clear thinking, spiritually evolved, and worthy of every drop of my admiration. After all, I "reasoned," he must be superior in many ways to have achieved so much. Once the meal and the conversation began, however, it did not take long for my admiration to fade. His anger, rooted of course in the fear and hate-filled neighborhood of his youth, was so overwhelming that it distorted his view of everything. He may have been bright, but personally and spiritually evolved he was not.

As he spewed invective after invective about how "all" the professors at Harvard were racist and how the content of the courses was little more than conservative propaganda, I just sat there in ill-disguised disillusionment as my Cobb salad wilted and my lemonade warmed to room temperature. Of course I probably never could have converted him to my point of view, but it sure would have been nice had I at least attempted, as Deborah did, to engage him in a conversation about why he felt the way he did. Here was a chance for me to dialogue on these issues, to show that I was willing to disagree with him and risk being accused of bias and white arrogance. Who knows, maybe if I had been honest, if I had been less patronizing, less a practitioner of Guerilla Bias, I would have been able to dampen his anger and show him that not all whites are racist, not every misspoken word is intended as an attack on his heritage, and that this new world he had worked so hard to enter is not as hostile as he thinks.

BENEFIT: RUMOR REDUCTION

Rumor, I'm sure you would agree, is the bane of the manager's life, and few subjects are as ripe for the rumor mill as diversity and the kinds of misunderstandings human difference can produce. We have all heard or been the victims of rumors like: "Have you heard that the CEO decided to let all the Muslims take off an hour early every day so they can go home to pray?" or "There's no doubt about it, they brought in that new vice president just because she's black, they are just trying to be politically correct" or "The only reason I can figure that Bob gave Joe that promotion is because they are both gay. I'll bet they have a thing going."

Unsubstantiated rumors like these play as big a role in perpetuating bias as real incidents that can at least be pinned down and, therefore, dealt with. Harvey, for example, was mangled in the rumor mill and would never have known it had his alleged victim not had one drink too many at a company reception. Bolstered by the courage found in her third glass of chardonnay, Jane, a member of Harvey's team, cornered him to talk about a rumor that had come her way. Apparently someone had overheard Harvey say that Jane was taking too much time off because of her children's illnesses. Deeply hurt, she said to Harvey, "Ever since I heard what you said, I have felt uncomfortable around you and have begun to wonder if you are treating me differently because I have kids to raise."

Harvey was shocked. He had great sympathy for Jane's responsibilities as a single mother of three children and had no memory of having said such a thing. As Jane and Harvey talked, as they walked together through their shared gateway, they sorted out what had happened. Harvey admitted he did have a conversation concerning Jane and her children, but had said nothing about her taking too much time off. What he had said, and this is what got distorted, was that her leaving, unavoidable as it was, was tough on her teammates. Of course it would have been better had Jane been able to enter this gateway conversation without benefit of chardonnay, but at least she did, and in the process she salvaged what was and, because of her forthrightness, continued to be a good working relationship.

Let me mention Tony Polk again to show how a little effort toward dialogue can clear up not only rumors but other types of misunderstandings as well. In this case, Tony was willing to take the risk of offending a neighbor to have a conversation about what he thought was a bias against him and his family:

> Tony, who now lives in a predominately white Virginia suburb, has a habit of working in his yard every day before heading off to work. He is not, however, the only one on his block with healthy early morning habits. Each morning Tony would see one of his neighbors striding by on his daily constitutional. Oddly—perhaps suspiciously—the man never spoke to Tony; not once in six months of early mornings did the neighbor even nod in Tony's direction, much less say hello. Accustomed to the reality of racism, Tony finally confronted the man and asked, "Why don't you ever speak to me? Is it because I'm black?" Surprised, the man answered, "No, not at all, I use my exercise as a time of reflection, everybody knows I don't talk to people when I'm walking."

Tony accepted this answer and was relieved. He also was glad he had risked asking; if he hadn't, he never would have known that in this case his assumption of racism had been wrong. It had all been an unfortunate misunderstanding.

BENEFIT: THE STIFLED SPREAD OF BIAS

As we saw elsewhere, bias is contagious. A perfect upbringing can inoculate against infection, but unfortunately, that strain of vaccine is in perilously short supply. Because of the shortfall of perfect upbringings, we need to face up to this fact:

The responsibility for stifling the spread of bias rests on each of us and our main method for achieving this goal is conversation.

There are many ways to talk about how this works, but you can't beat good old Pavlov and those dogs for giving us a clear explanation.

You may remember from high school that Pavlov's goal was to condition his dogs to salivate even in the absence of anything to salivate about. He created this reaction by setting off a buzzer and simultaneously giving the dogs meat powder. The meat powder, of course, made the dogs salivate. After a while, they would salivate when the buzzer went off even if the yummy powder failed to appear. If too much time went by without the powder being offered, however, the association between the sound and the treat wore off and the dogs no longer salivated when the buzzer was pushed.

People learn to be repelled by bias in exactly the same way that Pavlov's dogs learned to salivate at a sound. The only difference is that the dogs were conditioned by a positive reward (meat powder), while we are conditioned by a negative response (our parents' displeasure). As children, we witness or commit an inappropriate action (the buzzer goes off), our parents react critically (the meat powder appears), and we feel negative about that action and the bias it reflects (we salivate). As with the dogs, after several associations between the two (the inappropriate action and our parents' displeasure), we begin to feel negatively about bias (salivate) even if our parents aren't around to provide their input.

If, however, the negative reaction—from our parents, other people, or the culture at large—does not continue with reasonable consistency to accompany events involving bias, we eventually become deconditioned and no longer wince at inappropriate jokes, comments, or actions. Attitudes like, "Those Dominicans have no values, they are ruining the neighborhood" or "Gay people are just a bunch of perverts" or "Women are too emotional to be president" initially cause us to respond with repulsion and, hopefully, tempt us to say something in defense of these groups. But if we hear statements of bias often enough without the accompanying disdain of society, our repulsion becomes extinguished and we no longer regard them as particularly offensive. In short, we become insensitive to outrage (and the buzzer) and we no longer "salivate."

This is why it is our obligation to say something when a child or anyone else expresses a biased attitude. If the comment is met with a reprimand from the parent, children are more apt to see such statements as undesirable. I believe we know instinctively that this is the way words and their associations work. It is the reason we were so careful during the O.J. Simpson trial to avoid sounding out the word *nigger* even when just referring to it as a unit of vocabulary and employed, instead, the contrived but useful phrase "the 'n' word." It is the reason, too, that, as we saw elsewhere, bias cannot be tolerated from anyone, even from members of emerging groups; if bias is treated as somehow acceptable, no matter whose bias it is, the climate becomes compatible for its existence and for its spread. In short:

What we accept is what we teach.

CHAPTER SUMMARY

- Dialogue in the face of gateway events is one of the most effective tools for reducing bias.
- Open and honest conversation reduces bias by increasing mutual knowledge and understanding, minimizing and clarifying diversity-related rumors, and creating an atmosphere in which biased attitudes are unable to thrive.

11

GETTING DIVERSITY FIT

CHAPTER FOCUS QUESTION

How can I be prepared for a gateway event when it comes my way?

He couldn't call it anything other than an ambush or, if your taste runs to the medical, a "sudden onset" gateway event. It was early on a Monday morning and Jock was rushing to the weekly management meeting. Just as he rounded a corner he practically collided with two of his supervisors who were embroiled in a heated disagreement. As best he could figure it out, one of the combatants had offended the other with a comment about the new female sales associate. Knowing it was his job to do something, Jock stopped around the next turn, thought for a moment, then, as if he had come to some kind of a decision, moved on down the hall; after all, he couldn't be late for his meeting. "I just couldn't handle it," he told me, "I was caught off guard and decided to let the incident pass."

Most gateway events are like this, they swing open before us without warning. What this means is that we rarely have time to prepare a response or, for that matter, to sort out how we feel about what is going on. When this happens, we are in danger of walking away or, worse, going into autoresponder mode, spouting glib denials and politically correct nonsense. To prevent this kind of meltdown, we need to do what Jock did not do, prepare ahead of time for every contingency.

Much of what you have read so far in this book amounts to that preparation: Becoming mindful of your biases, weakening their impact, and learning to shove them aside are all part of your diversity fitness program. There is, however, one more workout that needs to be tackled to acquire—you guessed it—our desired "diversity hard body."

This final exercise entails naming and thus taming the emotions that accompany gateway conversations. We have talked about emotion a lot in these pages, most notably the fears that animate and drive our biases. The feelings we are after here, however, are of a different sort. In this context, we are concerned with those small and large terrors that compromise in several ways our ability to carry on effective conversations about bias.

- Fear interferes with our willingness to enter into the conversation in the first place.
- Fear prevents us from being able to think on our feet.
- Fear blocks our ability to interpret accurately what is going on.
- Fear pulls us out of the moment by tempting us to focus on painful experiences of the past or imagined disasters of the future rather than on the realities of the present.

If we are to be prepared to enter into gateway conversations and make them successful, we need to identify what it is we fear.

The ability to identify and observe an emotion is a cornerstone of emotional intelligence and greatly increases the chances of diminishing that emotion's impact on our ability to function.

It isn't necessary to exorcise our fears altogether, just giving them a name has a magical way of bringing the emotion under our control.

I learned the importance of identifying my own fears some years ago during a dinner with a new female acquaintance. Because my emotions were at that point still anonymous, they were utterly unchecked, cavorting around my mind in such a frenzy that they doomed what might have otherwise been a productive conversation. Here's the grizzly scene:

My dinner companion was a black woman named Candace who had just moved to town and whom I was anxious to welcome into the community. We met at a local restaurant—a restaurant, in fact, owned by Deborah, the woman who so effectively educated her sexist homophobic boss in an earlier chapter—and proceeded to have a great time talking "girl talk," being silly, comparing notes on the best shopping malls in town, and, most fun, trying to figure out how we were going to get her involved in the San Diego dating scene.

After about an hour of light conversation, we began to talk about my work and that led to what promised to be a most informative discussion about diversity. Unfortunately, that promise, as is often the case when we are afraid, was an empty one. Once the subject turned to race, we were transformed into different people. Gone were the play and shared interests; instead, we became a pair of women who were too self-conscious and defensive to carry on any kind of honest conversation.

Looking back, I realize we were both responsible for ruining the evening. Between our mutual defensiveness and shared failure to call attention to what was happening, we missed out on a prime opportunity to learn more about the complexities of human difference and how to make them work. All this because we were both afraid.

But what were we afraid of? If I had known that answer, I would have been able to analyze the fear and exorcise its power. Maybe you have some insights into what was going on.

Here is a list of some of the fears that you might have come up with in the Exploration Point at right:

- Fear of the intimacy (read honesty) and commitment that goes along with healthy conversation about bias: In this case, the issue was race. Bruce Jacobs says that it requires more intimacy to talk honestly about race than to have sex.[1] That may be overstating it a bit, but talking about race sure is a heck of a lot scarier than chatting about shopping malls and clothes.
- Fear of our own biases being revealed: Perhaps Candace was concerned that her bias toward white people might show through and damage a potential

E *x p l o r a t i o n*
P *o i n t*

Put yourself in my place or in Candace's— whichever role is most familiar to you (or both)— and try to identify the fears that kept each of us, and maybe you in the future, from bringing up the issue of race. What other fears and emotions might you have that could interfere with your ability to dialogue about bias?

friendship. Perhaps I was worried that biases of which I was barely aware might make an inopportune appearance in the form of a misspoken word or poorly chosen phrase.

- Fear of each other's anger: I'll admit that I did feel a little overwhelmed by Candace's personality. Was it just that she was charismatic, bright, and creative? If so, then it is certainly my problem. Or was there really anger there that might have come flooding out in an embarrassing display of emotion? If so, it was both our problems.
- Fear of appearing uptight, judgmental, or overly serious: Often when a gateway event is swinging open before us, we reach out to slam it shut for fear that if we bring up the "heavy" subject of bias, people will hurl back at us that most patronizing of all phrases, *lighten up.*

One of the purposes of this book is to encourage you to walk through gateway after gateway and learn more and more about diversity and bias and about yourself. As you turn the handle on each gate, you will no doubt come up against fears and reasons to hesitate that are not on this list. The more of these experiences you have in encountering, naming, and diffusing your fears, the easier the process will become and the more prepared you will be to take on any gateway event that comes your way.

CONCLUSION: PREPARING FOR THE NEXT STEP

E *x p l o r a t i o n* **P** *o i n t*

Before launching into the skills necessary to conduct good conversations when faced with gateway events, it is helpful to look back at how you have performed in the past. By answering these questions, you will have an idea of what your strong and weak points are and can thus better target your effort.

1. Think of one time when you had the opportunity to engage in a dialogue about bias but chose to walk away. Why did you hesitate?

2. Think of one conversation about bias in which you did participate but were not successful. What makes you think it was unsuccessful and what do you think you or the other parties did wrong?

3. Think of one incident in which you had a conversation following a gateway event that you consider successful. Why do you define the dialogue as successful? What were the elements in the conversation that made it work?

Getting Diversity Fit | 145

CHAPTER SUMMARY

- In order to participate successfully in gateway events, we need to name the fear that prevents us from dialoguing effectively.
- Fear not only makes us reluctant to talk about bias but also prevents us from thinking clearly, interpreting accurately what is going on, and focusing fully on the other participants in the conversation.
- The specific fears that accompany gateway events include fear of intimacy, fear of having our biases revealed, fear of either our or the other person's anger, or fear of being judged as excessively serious or "uptight."

12

COGNITIVE SKILLS FOR DIVERSITY DIALOGUE

CHAPTER FOCUS QUESTION

What cognitive skills do I need to carry on effective dialogue about a gateway event?

Do any of these situations seem familiar?

- You are a CEO who just gave an important speech regarding the goals for the next quarter. As you walk off the stage, one of your direct reports says she is offended by your comment that the company's new product would give the customer a real "bang for the buck." What do you do?
- You are a Diversity Manager who is conducting a pilot training program. Part of the course content deals with cultural differences in attitudes toward punctuality. In an attempt to contrast Latino notions of time with those found in mainstream American culture, you refer to the latter as "normal" with the implication that Latino views are "abnormal." No one catches your faux pas. What do you do?
- You are an American whose parents immigrated to the United States from China. While standing in the computer room at work, you overhear someone tell a joke about a Chinaman, a priest, and a rabbi. What do you do?

- You are a top-level manager who just hired a new assistant. In most ways she is great, but she does have a heavy accent that you sometimes can barely understand. You are concerned because your communication with her must be flawless. What do you do?

If you think you know how to deal with these sticky situations, you can skip right over this chapter. If, on the other hand, you look at each of these scenarios and get an uncomfortable feeling in the pit of your stomach and think, Gosh, I'm sure glad that hasn't ever happened to me, you had best read on.

This chapter provides the tools with which to handle situations like these as well as other types of gateway events. It begins with the general notion of taking a beat before reaching out and turning the handle on that gate, or, more likely, because of the amount of emotion that accompanies many gateway events, before kicking it open. The chapter then focuses on the following skills:

- How to set appropriate goals
- How to identify a shared enemy
- How to determine the contributions each person made to the event
- How to reduce gateway conversations to small and achievable units

RESIST, REMEMBER, RETHINK

Resist, remember, rethink. These three Rs sum up what our initial reaction should be to any gateway event. Think of these as the diversity version of those first three Rs: Reading, 'riting, and 'rithmetic.

Resist

Despite all the regulations that clearly state "two pieces per passenger," the people boarding after me were laden with packages and bags and so-called "carry-ons" that seemed too large to take on the *Titanic* much less onboard a SAAB 340B. I was absorbed in my reading, so I didn't see it coming: Bam! This huge dark green duffel bag swung around and hit me, hard, in the head. I looked up and with a scowl more appropriate to a deliberate attack than an act of clumsiness, struck back with an impatient, "Can't you be more careful?!" The woman who had lost control of the bag obviously had no intention of hitting me; nonetheless, my head hurt just as much as if it had been a carefully aimed assault and my response was just as churlish.

My defensive reaction to this surprise attack is exactly what happens at the outset of many gateway events. This is especially true if what has collided with one's psyche is an offensive comment or an accusation of bias. We initially recoil in surprise and then lash out. What we don't do is take a moment to regroup and assess what is really going on. We may feel hurt or offended or angry, but no matter what the genre of discomfort, an ill-considered response, even if it ends up being justified, will do more harm than good.

It is understandable that perceived attacks, and blows to the head, generate intense emotion. This intensity is why RESISTING is so important. The first thing we need to RESIST is the urge to vent the full force of our emotion. In this connection, there is a school of misguided thought that preaches: Once we have a feeling, we must express it. If we don't, the implication is, we will suffer some type of a psychological sprain that will take years to heal. The fact is:

It is not necessary to express every emotion we feel.

It is neither dishonest nor weak nor cowardly to stay in the moment and calm down before we react. It is, in fact, a very good idea. By calming down, we gain the objectivity that will allow us to communicate in a way that is most effective.

The second thing we need to RESIST is the urge to jump to conclusions about the intent of the actor. Right about now you might be asking this very pointed and slightly testy question: "Who cares about intentions? If I'm hurt, that's all that matters." Of course the impact of an act matters and that impact, if negative, must be remedied. The actor's intent, however, will help dictate that remedy and thus must be taken into consideration. The problem is if we jump to conclusions about intent and we are wrong, there is little chance of good conversation. Without conversation, there is no way we can assess intent. It is one of those circles that leads nowhere except to the destruction of any hope of resolving the situation.

As Douglas Stone, Bruce Patton, and Sheila Heen of the Harvard Negotiation Project say in their book *Difficult Conversations*, it is almost impossible to guess accurately a person's intentions. As they put it:

"Intentions are invisible. We assume them from other people's behavior. In other words, we make them up."[1]

We "make them up" largely according to the impact of the act on our welfare. When the Latino family was given a hotel room in a location far from the front desk, for example, they assumed the hotel staff intended to segregate them. Rather than RESIST the urge to jump to conclusions and, instead, take the time to consider another explanation, they complained of discrimination. What these guests didn't know was that they were given the remote location because that was the only way the hotel could accommodate their request for adjoining rooms; they were the only ones on the property. The family made an assumption based less on the realities of the moment than on a memory of past experiences in which they had, indeed, been discriminated against.

Remember

This brings us to the second of the three Rs. No matter what type of gateway event you find yourself in, ask yourself if the act or word that is bothering you seems familiar. If something has offended you, try to RE-MEMBER if the problematic action or word reminds you of a past experience with bias. Maybe, just maybe, you, like our Latino family, are responding to an earlier event rather than to the current one. Perhaps the pain you feel is coming not from the vice president you believe denied your promotion because of your ethnicity but from deep inside your own reservoir of unresolved slights and previous experience with discrimination. James, a gay man, used to do this all the time. It didn't matter that the person in question had never done a thing to harm him. That individual's innocence was irrelevant because others had been guilty. Because he couldn't strike back at the true bigots who attacked him in the past—they were out of range—he went after a third, and innocent, party who was closer at hand.

Frida, on the other hand, was successful at REMEMBERING the past when she encountered a gateway event on the first day of her new job. It happened when her boss repeatedly mentioned her Spanish language skills while introducing her around the office. The first time he did this, she recoiled from the remark and thought something like: Why is he dwelling on the fact I'm Latino? I sure hope he's not one of those bosses who values me only for my ethnicity. She was able, however, to RESIST the urge to say anything because she REMEMBERED that she had heard similar comments in the past from people who did in fact devalue her. Frida knew it was those comments that were causing her skepticism; they had nothing to do with this man, a man who, by the way, gave every sign of appreciating her for all she had to offer.

Frida also knew that we must stop prosecuting people like her boss for every real or imagined slip and that RESISTING and REMEMBERING are two excellent strategies for moving away from this habit of presuming people "guilty till proven innocent." Don't worry, if someone does something and we choose not to be offended and it turns out that we should have been, we will, unfortunately, always get another shot at outrage. Racism, sexism, and homophobia are rampant; there is still plenty of bias to go around. It is safe to take the risk of assuming the best and maybe, just maybe, the best will come to pass.

Another type of gateway event that is best met with a few moments of REMEMBERING is one in which we are accused of a bias. Most of us initially react to such accusations with quivering thoughts and utterances like, "I would *never* feel that way," "I would *never* stereotype," and, most certainly, "I would *never* look down on another group." Just as Frida and James needed to think back to past instances of abuse to avoid confusing them with the present, we, when accused of bias, have some REMEMBERING to do so we can see and evaluate the current event accurately:

- REMEMBER if anyone else has ever accused you of the same bias. If so, consider the possibility that both people are unlikely to be wrong.
- REMEMBER if you have a history of avoiding people from this kinship group, not hiring them, or saying things about them that you'd rather others not hear.
- REMEMBER how you feel when around this group. Do you feel at ease or is there a twinge of discomfort that just might be a clue to a biased attitude?

Perhaps after a few minutes of REMEMBERING, you will come out clean, or maybe not. In either case, you will know the truth of your motivations and be able to proceed with a conversation that is based on reality, not on a knee-jerk defensive response of the moment.

Rethink

Finally, we need to RETHINK what is going on. Think, for example, if you are accusing someone of a bias:

- Is the offending word or action unusual for the person you are indicting?

E *x p l o r a t i o n* **P** *o i n t*

Think back to a time when you were about to enter a gateway event. Were you able to RESIST, REMEMBER, and RETHINK? If so, how did the situation resolve itself? If not, how might those strategies have improved the situation? Having read this section, how might you handle such an event differently in the future?

- Has she done other things that support your reaction or, on the contrary, has she demonstrated that she respects and cares about people who are different from herself?
- If you have heard that she has done other things that might reflect a bias, are they merely rumors or are they events that you have witnessed and evaluated for yourself?

When we feel offended, the benefit of asking questions like these is enormous. That benefit is the acquisition of power. If we calmly examine what has happened, we gain the power that comes with objectivity. That power, in turn, grants us the option to either proceed confidently with our accusation or, alternatively, to shift our focus from the pain caused by the offense to the possibility of an unfortunate misunderstanding or an innocent act of clumsiness. See the Exploration Point above.

IDENTIFY YOUR GOALS

How a gateway event resolves itself is predicated only in part on the details of the initial action. The ultimate outcome is also influenced by the sequence of decisions that follow. The atrocity of September 11 was arguably the largest gateway event in U.S. history. The flash points on that event, however, lay not only in the attack itself but in each subsequent reaction to it. In short, each swing of the gate following an event provides another opportunity to make good or bad choices and to set good or bad goals.

One such choice following September 11 was the sending of an angry e-mail to an Islamic Web site. That e-mail read: "Go back to your beautiful land of sand and pig dirt, and take your HATE with you." Not so good so far: a brutal attack (gateway event) followed by a response that had the potential to make matters worse. Fortunately, the recipient of that e-mail, Mohammed Abdul Aleem, possessed the courage and goodness to react with compassion and kind words. That kindness, that spin-off gateway event, had the desired effect of soliciting an equally compassionate response from the angry and, as it turns out, frightened American who had sent the initial e-mail. The man replied with this apology: "I was upset by all the things that happened. My brother lost several of his friends at the Pentagon. I appreciate your calm and informative response . . . and as a result have since then come to my senses."[2]

The difference between these two correspondents is that one reacted rashly to the initial incident (September 11) while the other took the time to decide what he wanted to accomplish with his response. The first man's goals were vague at best: Did he just want to vent his emotion? Did he actually want to create more animosity with his angry words? Did he have the conscious intention to motivate Mr. Aleem and his friends to go back to the Middle East? We don't know, but the odds are pretty good that the American, if asked, would say that he had no idea what he was trying to accomplish by what he did; he just did it. Mr. Aleem's goals, on the other hand, were clear: His response was compassionate because his goal was restoring equanimity and good communication.

This electronic exchange illustrates the profound importance of setting goals before entering into dialogue. Diversity consultant Roosevelt Thomas says that:

"Dialogue is a conversation with a purpose."[3]

Aimless conversation, particularly if the catalyst for that conversation is emotionally charged, will lead nowhere or, worse, will lead somewhere you would rather not go. We need functional dialogue about bias, not just noise, and certainly not just conflict for conflict's sake.

Your specific goal or function will, of course, be shaped by the nature of the gateway event itself. The following is a sampling of the kinds of events you are most apt to encounter along with suggested goals. Keep this discussion in mind so that when each situation presents itself, you will be prepared and able to enter the dialogue with a firm function in mind.

You Feel Offended—What Is Your Goal?

When someone has done something we find offensive, it is our task and responsibility to communicate how we feel in a way that will accomplish our goals. I doubt it, but your goal might be to upset the person, make him angry, and hurt him like so many like him have hurt you before. Let's admit it, there is a certain pleasure in making people feel guilty. The problem is that "guilt-tripping" is a notoriously poor motivator of change. A little guilt served up gently might work, but too much can backfire and that backfire inevitably ignites a circle of destruction that spins something like this:

- The circle starts when a statement or act is perceived by someone as offensive.
- The person who feels hurt accuses the offender of bias and then says something with the intent of making him feel guilty.
- The "guilt-tripped" offender (who is now also a defendant) dislikes the accuser for making him feel guilty and, therefore, withdraws and becomes belligerent.
- The accuser perceives this belligerence as still more reason to be offended and redoubles her efforts to make the offender feel guilty.
- The offender (who, by the way, is rapidly taking on the role of victim) again withdraws.
- The accuser perceives this withdrawal as . . . etc., etc.

I told you the circle would spin; even my head is spinning from trying to figure out how all this jousting works. Setting a goal of guilt and revenge doesn't seem like a very good idea to me.

My friend Barbara Ceconi, whom you met earlier, was, she admits, tempted to go down the rocky road to revenge when she encountered a man on the street who found it entertaining, or felt it was his moral obligation or some other such foolishness, to call her a lesbian. Barbara, as you know, is blind and was walking with a female friend who was guiding her by the arm. As the man walked past the pair, Barbara heard him mutter, "Look at those lesbians flaunting their homosexuality. It's disgusting."

When Barbara heard this barely audible attack, she had a choice to make and a goal to set. Barbara's chosen goal would depend on the answers to two questions:

1. What did she want to accomplish?
2. Was there a reasonable chance of her accomplishing that goal without paying too high a price? In other words, was it worth it?

One goal Barbara might have had in speaking to this man is a sometimes sweet one: revenge. Make him feel bad. Imagine his humiliation at being accosted in public by a blind woman and berated for calling her a lesbian. If Barbara wanted to feel better by causing pain, this certainly was achievable, but it also would compromise a more important long-term goal:

To educate others about how people with disabilities should be regarded and treated.

It is impossible to know if Barbara could have succeeded at educating this particular person—that would have been determined by the nature of the man and the virulence of his fear. Her odds for success, however, would have soared if she approached him with compassion and with an eye toward preserving both her dignity and his. Knowing what I do of Barbara, that is just how she would have gone about it. Barbara knows that people are far more apt to listen if they are not distracted by efforts to build an emotional fire wall with which to protect themselves against attack.

E *x p l o r a t i o n*
P *o i n t*

Think back to a time when you were offended by someone's comment or action. What goal did you set for the conversation that followed? Having read this section, what goals might you set for the future?

You Have Been Rightly Accused of Bias— What Is Your Goal?

I am now casting you in the role of the man who offended Barbara so deeply. You have continued on down the street, sure of yourself in your moral judgment, completely oblivious to the fact that this "lesbian" and her friend are hot on your heels. Much to your dismay, you feel a tap on your shoulder and turn around to find yourself staring straight into the faces of two very angry women. They proceed, following as much RESISTING, REMEMBERING, and RETHINKING as they can muster, to explain your mistake.

Your first instinct in a situation like this will be to defend yourself. Obviously you must think you are right or you wouldn't have committed the offending act in the first place. This book, however, is all about awareness and each of us, even when in the midst of an embarrassing gateway event, must strive toward one simple goal:

To remain aware and open enough to consider the possible truth of the accusation.

This means that we must, first, really listen to what the accuser has to say and, second, take a turn at a round of RESISTING, REMEMBERING, and RETHINKING. Ask yourself: Is there a grain of truth to the accusation? When you approached your three coworkers and only shook hands with the two Asians, did part of you intend to slight the white

E *xploration*
P *oint*

Think back to a time when you were rightly accused of a biased attitude. Upon learning of that accusation, what goal did you set for the conversation? Having read this section, what goals might you set in the future?

man? When you made that joke about all men being sexist, was it really just a joke or was your colleague justified in recoiling under the force of your stereotype? Consider these possibilities. You might learn something interesting about yourself.

You Have Been Wrongly Accused of Bias—What Is Your Goal?

Let's say you have been accused of a bias, really listened to what the other person had to say, really thought it out, and are convinced that the accusation is wrong. What on earth is your goal then? I can best answer this question by telling you what happened to my colleague Gayle who is, as you can see from this incident, very skilled at handling awkward gateway events.

Gayle, an experienced diversity trainer, was about halfway through conducting a workshop when he had occasion to refer to the "flip" chart that stood in the corner of the room. No sooner was the word out of his mouth when a hand shot up. "How can you, a diversity trainer, be so insensitive? 'Flip,'" the irate woman said, "is a pejorative term for Filipino."

Yes, flip is a pejorative term for Filipino, but it is also the name of a large pad of paper mounted on an easel. Gayle would agree with me that if we carry the accuser's thinking—that an offensive word is inappropriate even if used for an entirely different purpose—to its logical conclusion, women would be right to protest every reference to baby "chicks," gay people to become angry at the very mention of anything that is "queer," and people with disabilities to express outrage when a golfer refers to her "handicap." Faced with such distorted reasoning, Gayle had a couple of options. He could set a goal of making the accuser feel justified (and end up looking like a good guy in the deal). To accomplish this, he would have to pretend that the accusation was correct and fake an apology (that means, lie). A corollary result of this misguided goal would be that the accuser would remain ignorant of her mistake and continue to chronically find offense where none existed.

On the other hand he could set a goal to:

Hold the accuser to a high standard of judgment.

This is exactly what Gayle did. He thanked the woman for her comment and respectfully pointed out that the term *flip* had only one possible meaning in the context in which it was used. Gayle said that he was sorry if the comment made her uncomfortable, but he did not actually apologize for having said it. He, instead, held his accuser to a high standard of intelligence and understanding. He even respected her enough to ask if she'd like to discuss the matter a bit more during the break.

E *x p l o r a t i o n*
P *o i n t*

Think back to a time when you were falsely accused of a biased attitude. Upon learning of that accusation, what goal did you set for the conversation? Having read this section, what goal would you set for the next time?

You Are Speaking with Someone with Whom You Disagree—What Is Your Goal?

Fortunately, I had firm goals in mind when my colleague, a woman named Liz, presented me with a gateway event that was triggered by a disagreement over the appropriate use of language:

> The conversation took place following a presentation in which I mentioned the case of Gayle and his "flip" chart. After the session, I ran into Liz in the hallway of the hotel. When she saw me, she nodded and continued on her way. After a few steps, however, she seemed to change her mind about something, turned back, and asked if I had a few minutes to talk. We sat down on a bench against the wall and, with great courtesy and some hesitation, she told me that she strongly disagreed with my position about the appropriateness of the word *flip*.

Liz and I talked for about 15 minutes. Did she convince me of her point of view? No, she didn't. Did I convince her of mine? Not at all. Fortunately, neither of us had that as the goal of the conversation. The goal was not, nor does it need to be, to convince the other person of your view. Our purpose, instead, was to talk about an issue that affected our work and our lives. One thing I learned from this conversation is that two perspectives can exist together in the universe without an explosion and that open dialogue is as noble an achievement and as appropriate a goal as consensus.

RECOGNIZE A COMMON ENEMY

It was the night of the Los Angeles riots, April 1992. I lived in San Diego but was vividly aware of the chaos that reigned 135 miles up the coast. Between phone calls from frenzied relatives and lurid television coverage, it seemed that my childhood home-town had turned into an inferno of hatred and violence. Finally, it all got to be too much so my husband and I decided to drive down to the local mall in a futile effort to escape reality.

The mall was deserted except for a few other couples who, like us, were ambling from shopwindow to shopwindow. I recall one couple in particular. The only reason I remember them is the color of their skin and that color was black. As we passed within a few feet of each other, I swear there was unspoken com-munication between us. My silent contribution to the conversa-tion were questions like: "Do you think I'm racist because I'm white?" "Are you angry with me too?" "Do you think I'm afraid of you?" Their questions were: "Do you hate me for what is going on in LA?" "Are you afraid of me?" "Are you resentful of me and the color of my skin?"

How wonderful it would have been had we been able—I should say, willing—to approach one another and discuss the horror of what was going on. Had we done so, we would have discovered that we shared something very profound: a common foe.

In every situation in which there is conflict around difference, there is, by definition, a common enemy and that enemy is a shared culture of bias that tricks and seduces us into misunderstanding and mistrust. No matter what genre of gateway event might bring us into a conver-sation about bias, no matter how different we seem and how separate our stance, we share the sad reality that we both have been injured by the same adversary. Some of us have injuries more severe than others; some have fatal wounds, some mere contusions; but, no matter what the degree:

We have all been damaged by the existence of bias in our culture.

Perhaps you are damaged because of disadvantages resulting from your gender or sexual orientation. Perhaps you have had little bias directed against you, but are a victim just the same because your own biases have deprived you of rich relationships and fruitful experiences. Maybe you are a victim because the prevalence of bias has led to false accusations against you or maybe you are an innocent bystander caught in a crossfire of fear and conflict. No matter who we are and no matter what our perspective, bias is an enemy we all share. The more we shift our emphasis during conversations from fighting each other to fighting the common foe, the more productive those conversations will become.

Candace and I should have done this. As I think back, our shared enemy was right there, perched on the barstool next to us, whispering historical truisms artfully interspersed with lies and distortions into our ears, creating fear, and hesitation, and distrust. Had we had the presence of mind to call out the enemy, to name her, and to say to each other, "Wow, isn't this weird? Before we began talking about race, we were having fun. Now that the subject of bias has come up, we're all self-conscious and tongue-tied. I wonder what's going on."

Candace and I, two intelligent and educated women, could have outmatched the demon, but we allowed the foe to divide us and that was our fatal mistake. Candace and I were both prisoners of the bias wars, under siege in the same stone fortress, listening to the same propaganda. Rather than recognize that reality and join our skills to concoct an escape plan, we fought each other. Tony and Dennis didn't make that mistake; they identified the enemy, stood on each other's shoulders and scaled the wall to freedom.

RECOGNIZE MUTUAL CONTRIBUTIONS

Every gateway event is a collaborative effort. One of the parties might hold the moral high ground and be more right than the other, but both people, by virtue of the fact that they were present, must in some way have contributed to the friction. Notice that I say "contributed"; this has nothing to do with blame, guilt, or innocence, or with who should be rightfully punished. If I leave my purse on the front porch and someone takes it, I am certainly not to blame, but my absentmindedness was a contributing factor to the fact that the bag was stolen.

Here is an example of how two people contributed to a gateway event that might have turned ugly and expensive. It started when Nonna accused Rachel, her manager, of bias against her and the other Russian immigrants in the department. When Rachel heard the accusation, she was initially shocked. After talking to Nonna, however, she realized that they shared equal responsibility for the negative feelings between them:

> As it turns out, Nonna, since arriving in the United States, had experienced discrimination at every turn. Because of these bad experiences, she developed the habit of seeing bias even where none existed. For her part, Rachel tended to stay to herself, rarely mixed with her colleagues, and never socialized with them outside of work. On top of that, she admitted to having difficulty understanding her Russian-born team members' accents and, because she was uncomfortable, avoided having conversations on the plant floor.

Between Rachel's natural coolness and Nonna's sensitivity to perceived bias, it is no wonder there was tension. This is a case of two women, both innocent, and yet both contributors to a tension that could have proved painful and expensive.

Obviously, an important element in any good conversation following a gateway event is the willingness to admit your own contribution. This means to be self-aware and honest. Let's face it, when it comes to talking about bias, a lot of lying goes on around the edges, a skirting of the truth that slows us down and serves only to make matters worse. Here are some examples of the kinds of honest admissions that will guarantee a far more productive dialogue:

- If you have contributed to a gateway event by accusing someone of sexism, admit you tend to see sexism a lot because of past experiences. This admission does not automatically mean your accusation is wrong; it does, however, communicate your willingness to talk honestly and openly.
- If someone has accused you of bias, admit you grew up in a racist community and still might not be completely free of its message. Again, this admission does not automatically mean you are guilty, only that you are aware of past influences on your thinking.
- If someone has expressed concern about your attitude toward gay people, admit that you may have contributed to that perception because you are a little uncomfortable with those who have a different sexual orientation than your own. This is not an admission of homophobia, only a sign of your willingness to explore the issue from all angles.

- If you don't understand someone's point of view—if you don't "get it"—say so. This admission has the power of communicating both your willingness to learn and your interest in understanding the other person's perspective.

We need to acknowledge our contribution at every opportunity. Sure, every once in a while, the other person will take our inch of admission and stretch it into a distorted mile in which the truth is hardly recognizable or, worse, she will use it as a shield to keep from seeing her own role in the event. Usually, however, people respond positively to the gift of vulnerability and in turn become more willing to look at and confess their own share of responsibility. See the Exploration Point below.

Here are some thoughts on Cindy's and Horace's mutual contributions to the problem:

- Cindy has the right to exclude anyone she wants from her meetings. The fact that she didn't include Horace is, nonetheless, a contributing factor to the situation.
- Cindy further contributed by failing to tell Horace of her policy about who does and does not attend board meetings.
- Horace, on the other hand, contributed by jumping to a conclusion about Cindy's motivation; he never even considered asking why he had been excluded.

Another way in which we each might contribute to a gateway event is by bringing to it differing communication styles. Although we can't generalize about any group of people, there are differences in the way some men and some women communicate. Those differences are at times delightful, but they can also lead to tension and misunderstanding. Here is an example that will seem familiar. As you read it, give some

---

E x p l o r a t i o n **P** o i n t

Cindy, president of a largely female-staffed cosmetics firm, failed to invite Horace, her new administrative assistant, to the weekly board meeting. Not realizing that it had always been Cindy's policy to exclude support staff from these meetings, Horace complained of sexism and unfair treatment.

Both people contributed to the situation. On the basis of these few details, can you identify the role that each played in creating this gateway event?

thought to the role each party played in creating the tension. Reminder: This is not an issue of guilt or innocence, merely contribution.

> Sharon presents an idea at a departmental meeting. Her supervisor, Joe, interrupts her and says that he feels her idea is not well thought out and that he has a better one. Without returning the floor to Sharon, he proceeds to outline his plan.
>
> When Joe finishes speaking, Sharon says that she can understand his point of view then asks him some questions about his ideas. She then picks up where she left off before being interrupted. She begins by saying, "I think Joe's idea is great and maybe some of you will disagree with this, but I think I might have a better solution." After she finishes her thoughts, Sharon asks the group for feedback.
>
> Two weeks following this meeting, Joe has to make a decision about whether or not to promote Sharon to a more responsible position. He decides against it. When the word gets out that Sharon did not get the job, rumors spread that Joe discriminated against her because she is a woman; a gateway event is born.

Joe did not deliberately discriminate against Sharon; he did, however, contribute to the problem and so did she:

- Sharon contributed to this gateway event through her communication style. Like many women, Sharon softened her statements and her stance. She did this by spreading credit around, inviting feedback, asking questions, and adding tentative phrases to her statements.
- Joe contributed by bringing his own ideas about what Sharon's tentative communication style meant about her leadership abilities: Joe believed she lacked the confidence necessary for such an important management position.
- Joe's "all-man" communication style was another contributing factor. His directness and abruptness led Sharon and others at the meeting to see him as disrespectful of her views. This perception added fuel to the rumor that Joe had a bias against women.

Both Joe and Sharon played roles in this event. If they, and people like them, had been willing to claim responsibility for those roles, the situation could have been seen for what it was—a misunderstanding, rather than an illegal and immoral act of discrimination.

BUILD ON THE PYRAMID PRINCIPLE

It was February of 1999 when I sat in my hotel room in Cairo, feet up on the sill, whiskey glass in hand, gazing out the window at one of the most amazing sights on the planet: the Great Pyramid of Cheops. Looming in the mist, it seemed grander and more elegant than its likeness in even the most touched-up travel photograph.

I wasn't thinking much about bias reduction on that romantic night, but the image of the pyramid stayed with me and laid the foundation for what I call the Pyramid Strategy for succeeding at gateway conversations. This strategy is informed by what any architect knows about building: whether it is constructing the Pyramid of Cheops or Blenheim Palace or the Vatican or the Great Wall of China, the only way to proceed is one stone at a time.

When it comes to conversations about bias, this means we need to adopt the motto:

"Think small."

Often in the heat of a gateway event, we become overloaded by the scope of the issue and the intensity of emotion. That overload can, in turn, leave us paralyzed and unable to act. The trick to popping the clutch and getting moving again is to sidestep the main issue of the conflict for a moment—don't worry, you'll get back to it later—and, instead, build a foundation of small successes on which the solution to the big problem can ultimately rest. By thinking smaller, we create bite-size strategies that can be swallowed without gagging and that are manageable even when we are lost in a maze of self-consciousness, anger, or fear.

Looking back on my ill-fated lunch with the Harvard graduate, I realize I could have used the Pyramid Strategy to make progress toward better communication with this fascinating young man. There was no way that we were going to leap to mutual understanding and trust in the span of one Cobb salad and a lemonade, but we could have taken a few tentative steps in that direction.

For one thing, we might have admitted our discomfort and thereby cracked open the door to better dialogue: *stone number one.*

We then might have agreed to take turns talking for short periods without interruption or reprisal from the other: *stone number two.*

We might also have made a pact that should one person not understand something, he or she would ask for clarification: *stone number three.*

And wider and wider the base becomes and firmer the foundation until we have constructed, if not the Great Pyramid of Cheops, at least a modest structure of good communication with the potential of understanding.

CHAPTER SUMMARY

- It is important to collect our thoughts and feelings before proceeding with a gateway conversation. In this way, we maximize the likelihood of accurately assessing the dynamics of the situation and, therefore, of proceeding appropriately.
- Setting goals before entering into a gateway event increases the chances of achieving a positive outcome.
- Within every gateway event, both parties share the common enemy of bias. Bias permeates our culture and affects us all in different ways.
- Gateway conversations are more apt to end successfully if we recognize the contributions of all participants.
- Gateway events are best resolved by breaking them into small units that can be resolved in easily achievable stages.

13

VERBAL SKILLS FOR DIVERSITY DIALOGUE

CHAPTER FOCUS QUESTION

What verbal skills do I need to carry on effective dialogue about a gateway event?

PeeWee Reese, captain of the Brooklyn Dodgers in the 1940s and 1950s, knew nothing about the rules of political correctness the day he faced an angry crowd on a baseball field in Louisville, Kentucky. Despite his lack of sophistication and his being a child of his times, PeeWee's language was one of highest respect and compassion. As taunts of "Jungle Bunny" and "Snowflake" hurled down on Jackie Robinson, PeeWee quietly walked from his position at shortstop and put an arm around Jackie's shoulder. PeeWee, a slight man, a white man, and a Southerner, said not one word. His elegant gesture permeated and diluted the climate of hatred more effectively than the most effusive of tirades. Jackie, by the way, got the message too. His response? "I never felt alone on a baseball field again."[1]

PeeWee's eloquence had nothing to do with using the latest terminology or the most precise pronoun. PeeWee was a good communicator; he was a good communicator because he knew his audience and he knew that rhetorical overkill would only make this gateway event spiral down into a morass of racial hatred and violence. He also knew that the language chosen needed to be simple: an arm around the shoulder; enough said.

The purpose of this chapter is to help us all learn to communicate as well and as eloquently as PeeWee Reese. In Chapter 12 we focused on the cognitive and emotional skills we need to reach that goal. In this chapter, we will turn our attention to the words themselves—which ones we choose and how they should be spoken. The topics include the importance of:

- Avoiding vocal and verbal hyperbole
- Minimizing dogmatic language
- Maintaining high standards in how we communicate
- Using creative communication strategies
- Listening

EMPLOY VERBAL AND VOCAL MODULATION

The communication principle that PeeWee understood more than any other is the importance of modulation. In radio, modulation means to adjust the phase, frequency, or amplitude of a transmission to a level that will most successfully carry the broadcast. In human communication, and no more than in the emotionally charged context of gateway events, modulation means to lower our verbal and vocal volume to ensure that our message is heard.

My father, who was an actor, taught me something important about the presentation of dialogue, ideas, or accusations:

Lower your voice.

By softening our ideological and physical voices to a whisper, we allow, and even tempt, the listener to crane forward to hear, and more readily understand, what this mysterious and barely audible message is all about. As my father used to say, "A whisper is more tantalizing and a lot more interesting than a shout." While loud and harsh utterances cause most of us to retreat behind a soundproof wall of denial and disinterest, a softer tone has a remarkable way of creating a feeling of safety for and, thus, receptivity in the listener.

This lowering of "volume" applies not just to how loud we speak but also to the intensity of the words we use. Admittedly, verbal modulation is tough for many Americans because our culture loves large language.

We like to indulge in a kind of overspeak in which the finest eggs are always the biggest, buildings the tallest, and movies the highest grossing. This is all very nice when pitching a product or coming up with a book title that sells, but exaggeration is a surefire way to draw psychological blood—inflaming the dialogue to the point of conflagration or, worse, shutting down the conversation entirely.

Many of us believe that for words to be effective, they must be forceful, dramatic, and exaggerated. The opposite is true:

Understatement is almost always more powerful and often more accurate than exaggeration.

Assume for the moment that someone has offended you and your goal is to help reduce any bias he may have, or, at the very least, motivate him to stop and think next time around. You will have a far better chance of accomplishing this goal if you avoid using exaggerated terms, or what is referred to as "hyperbole."

Unfortunately, anger and stress tempt us to use emotionally charged words such as *racist, sexist,* and *homophobic.* Homophobic, for example, is a clinical term meaning "a pathological obsession with homosexuality caused by the heavily suppressed fear that one may be homosexual oneself." Wouldn't you agree that a "pathological obsession" is absurd hyperbole when applied to what happened to Betsy when her officemate expressed surprise that she was gay? We accomplish only one thing when we spread such potent words around so liberally: we weaken the impact of our message.

Another problem with the use of hyperbole is that it gives the accused justification to play the innocent. Most people associate words such as racist with lynchings, homophobic with hate crimes, and sexist with the desire to keep women barefoot and pregnant. That's not me, the defendant is apt to think with relief, and most of the time he'll be right if measured by what those words have traditionally meant. If the terms of attack were more reasoned, if the crime of which we accuse someone were pled down to a misdemeanor, then maybe we could maintain an atmosphere in which a productive conversation could take place. As psychologist Paul Wachtel says in *Race in the Mind of America:*

Accusing a guilty man of the wrong crime is one of the greatest gifts one can bestow upon him. It fosters an orgy of self-righteous conviction of innocence, and conveniently diverts his attention from the offense of which he is truly guilty.[2]

Cranking up the emotional volume, which is what hyperbole is all about, provides no assurance that your message will be heard. It instead guarantees that the accused, whether guilty or innocent, will be sorely tempted to cover her ears, learn nothing, and turn and walk away.

A much better solution to ill-treatment is to couch our complaints in terms of behaviors rather then labels. Here are two approaches to the same gateway event. Read them over and contrast them in terms of their effectiveness at achieving the desired goal of good communication and behavior change:

1. *Approach A:* Rachel, having worked for months with a boss who treated her poorly, walked into his office, sat down, and said: "I'm really tired of your *sexist* treatment. You ignore my ideas, never give me feedback, and have regularly excluded me from key meetings. I hope things change or I'll have no choice but to go to Human Resources with a complaint."

2. *Approach B:* Rachel, having worked for months with a boss who treated her poorly, walked into his office, sat down, and said: "I'm really tired of your treatment. You ignore my ideas, never give me feedback, and have regularly excluded me from key meetings. I hope things change or I'll have no choice but to go to Human Resources with a complaint."

In terms of language, these two statements differ by just one word: sexist. In terms of effectiveness, they differ by far more than that. In Approach A, Rachel labels her boss's behavior and makes an assumption about his attitude and intentions—he is, she has decided, sexist. Of course it is possible, even likely, that he does have a sexist attitude, but Rachel can't know that for sure. Because she doesn't know it for sure, there is no point in using the word. All her use of an inflammatory label will accomplish is to make her boss defensive and angry. Rachel's goal of changing her boss's behavior, and maybe even his attitude, would be better served by adhering to the proven facts: the man doesn't treat her right, period.

E *x p l o r a t i o n*
P *o i n t*

Why would Approach B be more effective in achieving Rachel's goal of changing her boss's behavior?

AVOID DOGMATIC LANGUAGE

Another language choice that can interfere with our conversational goals is the use of dogmatic or absolute statements. Have you ever been in a discussion in which one person rebuts an argument with, "Well, that's the law" or "It's in the Bible" or "That's what I was taught"? End of conversation and, most important, end of learning. Of course, we have every right to believe in the law or the Bible or in what our parents taught us. What we don't have is the right to use these beliefs as devices to stop the dialogue. Slamming the ideological lid on a topic might make us feel righteous and safe, but it is also an excellent way to defeat our goals of sustaining productive conversation, getting to know each other better, and pounding another nail into the coffin of bias.

It is when someone has accused us of a biased attitude that we are most tempted to make dogmatic statements. Particularly if we haven't gotten ourselves diversity fit, we are apt to buckle at the knees and at the heart, and lash back with an inflexible, "Well, that's too bad, that's just how I feel" or "You're too sensitive" or that pair of old standbys: "You know what I meant" and "I was only kidding." Each of these dismissive phrases does little more than make the accuser feel diminished and the accused look—and probably be—foolish.

Gayle, no doubt, would have studiously avoided all these phrases. You recall from the last chapter that he is the one who was accused of bias for using the term *flip* during a training session. After respectfully explaining the context in which he used the word, Gayle invited his accuser to discuss the issue during a break. Although we are not privy to that conversation, my guess is that Gayle resisted the urge to make any inflexible statements that would have served only to stop the discussion and make himself appear defensive. See the Exploration Point.

Had we been eavesdropping, we might have heard Gayle say things like:

- "You have a different perspective, I'd like to hear more."
- "Thanks for speaking up about how you feel. We need more open discussions like this."
- "I'm sorry you feel that way, what makes you say that?"

Admittedly, open-ended, nondogmatic statements and questions like these do take a little courage to utter. That is because they just might produce a rich conversation in which honest emotions and ideas are exchanged; kind of scary, but very much worth the risk.

E x p l o r a t i o n P o i n t

What phrases might Gayle have used during the conversation?

MAINTAIN A HIGH STANDARD

Like dogmatic statements, sinking to the other person's level may seem like a good idea at the time, but it will always turn out to be a mistake. Helen is a good example of how a nice person can be sucked into the verbal mire by the bias around her:

> Helen, who worked in a male-dominated manufacturing environment, had had enough. Day after day, week after week, she was exposed to a litany of comments such as "It must be that time of the month" or "She must not be getting enough."
>
> One day at a departmental meeting, Helen's male supervisor blew his top over a proposed change in procedures. Helen decided to seize the opportunity to help her boss understand how women feel when their emotions are dismissed as hormonal hallucinations and responded by saying, "You know, Jack, you're getting awfully emotional. I guess it must be that time of the month."

This approach might have been mildly amusing if Helen and Jack had been two friends kibitzing at a dinner party or a football game. They were, however, in the workplace and that meant that the comment was inappropriate at best and destructive at worst. See the Exploration Point.

You guessed it; her disrespectful comment backfired. All it did was reinforce her colleagues' belief that women found such comments amusing. It also strengthened their bias that women somehow deserve or want to be treated like second-class citizens. What it didn't do was reduce the ill-treatment to which Helen was subjected.

E *x p l o r a t i o n*
P *o i n t*

What impression do you think Helen's comments left on her colleagues? What information did it convey? How might her response increase rather than decrease the bias in her workplace?

STRIVE FOR CREATIVE COMMUNICATION

Using respectful language is important, but it also needs to be language to which the other person can relate. An analogy, for example, is a great tool for helping someone grasp, and even agree with, your point of view. I learned this technique during a mild gateway event involving my husband and myself. It happened when I realized that Tom was failing to grasp why having the confederate flag flying over the South Carolina courthouse was upsetting to some black Americans. He just couldn't get it. He kept coming back at me with arguments like "But the flag symbolizes more than just slavery," "It was so long ago," and "It doesn't mean that anymore." Finally, I realized I needed to talk about this issue in terms that connected to his own kinship group. I decided to exploit the fact that Tom is three-quarters Swedish. Here's my side of the conversation:

> Tom, assume for the moment that the Swedes were enslaved by the Norwegians until the middle of the 19th century. Also assume that, during that time, the Norwegians had a flag that symbolized in part their stand that they had the right to own slaves and that Norwegians were innately superior to the Swedes. Eventually, let's say, the Norwegians were forced by the Danes to free the Swedes, but continued to use the flag as a symbol of their history and identity. Now, how would you feel about seeing that symbol on the top of your own government buildings?

Need I say more? Tom got it.

REALLY LISTEN

Booker Izell, currently vice president of diversity at the *Atlanta Journal*, has much to teach us about the verbal side of dialoguing about diversity and the power that such dialogue has in reducing bias. Booker travels a great deal and one day he had the misfortune—or at least it initially looked like a misfortune—to sit next to a deeply biased man on the airplane:

> The man was upset by an article he had just read about crime in the black community and said something to Booker about blacks acting like animals. Sensing a gateway event in the offing and keeping his cool, Booker responded with, "You do know I'm black, don't you?" Undeterred and remarkably unembarrassed, his seatmate responded with, "Oh, you're OK, but I think we should send the bad ones back to Africa."
> The man was talking so loudly that the flight attendant became concerned and offered Booker another seat. Much to her surprise, and certainly to the surprise of Booker's seatmate, he

refused the attendant's offer, saying, "I want to hear this. I want to listen to his point of view." The two men talked for the entire length of the flight. After they landed and retrieved their carry-on luggage from the overhead rack, the man reached out to shake Booker's hand and said, "I enjoyed talking to you. I may not change, but you really have given me food for thought."

Booker, and his willingness to listen, just may have started this man down the road to something good. Booker knew how to listen; he knew that listening means to stay present—in the moment—listening only to the person in front of you. This wasn't easy for him because dozens, if not hundreds, of other white men were horning in on this mile-high conversation. Those interlopers were the racist men who had previously made Booker feel small and "less than" and diminished because of his color. But Booker had the moral strength to exclude these others from the dialogue and listen only to the one human being who sat beside him.

Judging from the success of this conversation, I would bet that Booker abided by another cardinal rule of good listening: No cross talk allowed. *Cross talk* is a term used at Alcoholic Anonymous meetings and refers to the rule that allows each person to talk without interruption or rebuttal. By refraining from cross talk, the full breadth of the speaker's thoughts and emotions can be laid on the table. I used to do this with my daughter. We had a ritual in which she and I invited the other to indulge in a good "vent." This meant allowing an unbroken stream of emotion and words to pour out without criticism or response. Venting sessions like these encourage and allow emotions to be expressed, and when it comes to reducing bias, understanding emotions is important. As the authors of *Difficult Conversations* point out, if you don't listen to emotions, "You'll get the plot, but not the point."[3]

Unfortunately, when we talk about something that involves a difference of opinion, as is the case with many gateway events, we tend not to listen. This is because we believe that really listening gives the impression that we agree with our opponent. In fact, eloquent listening sends only one message: that we care about resolving the situation. George, Charmaine's boss, delivered this message at a time when she desperately needed to hear it:

> When Charmaine was passed over for a promotion, she went to George and accused him of homophobia. At the start of the conversation, she was very emotional, not just because of the loss of this one promotion, but also because she had recently

been the victim of two layoffs. She felt vulnerable, abused, and a little frightened. As George heard Charmaine's complaints, he knew her charges were false, but, nonetheless, he fell silent and listened. When Charmaine was finished, George understood how frustrated she was and why she might have mistaken workplace realities for discrimination.

If George had refused to listen, if he had succumbed to anger or defensiveness and begun to jabber on about how wrong Charmaine was, he never would have gained that knowledge. As it was, he was able to empathize with her frustrations, explain the situation, avoid costly litigation, and retain a valuable employee to boot.

CONCLUSION: LIVING ANYWHERE WE WANT

Obviously, Tony and Dennis didn't need any of the techniques discussed in these last two chapters. Good conversation came naturally to them. It has been 50 years since that first encounter in college and they are still friends. Dennis, in fact, writes Tony often and teases him with the question, "Are you living next to any white people yet, Tony?" Politically correct? Of course not. Friends? Absolutely.

Tony's answer, by the way, to Dennis's 50-year-old question, "Why do you want to be with whites anyway?" was, "It's not that I necessarily want to be with white people, I just want to get an education so I can live anywhere I want."

CHAPTER SUMMARY

- Lowering the "volume" of both tone and words increases interest in what we have to say, maximizes credibility, and minimizes resistance to our message.
- It is tempting to make absolute or dogmatic statements in the heat of a gateway event. Although we all have the right to believe as we do, such statements only serve to shut down conversation and create defensiveness.
- One of the biggest mistakes we can make when talking about diversity is to respond in kind when someone speaks to us with disrespect. Always maintain high standards of communication.

- Not every person we converse with shares our values or life history. When attempting to get your message across, use metaphors, analogies, and similes to address that individual in a way they can most readily understand.
- Listening attentively and openly is perhaps the single most important aspect of dialoguing about diversity.

Conclusion

M o m e n t   o f   T r u t h

Each morning—well, most mornings—I roll out of bed and stagger into a room in my house that is variously called "the meditation room," "Little Man's room" (that's my grandson, Aiden), or, in homage to my stepdaughter who once slept there, "Krista's room." I call the dog, plop myself on the floor in an awkward and painfully unnatural cross-legged sit, ring the meditation bell, and begin to do battle with my mind. That's where the dog comes in, her rhythmic breathing and inspiring ability to take life as it comes serve as a constant, if at times noisy, reminder of what I am trying to accomplish.

Last week, my mind and I were engaged in a particularly bloody skirmish when I had one of those forehead-slapping insights that escape notice when one is drowning in the minutia of life. In a flash I realized that the goal of these meditations—to take life one breath, one thought, one experience at a time—is as pertinent to reducing bias as it is to living a happier, more fulfilling existence.

As we have seen in the pages of this book, biases are distorted views of other human beings that are created by messages from the past and sustained by fear of what will happen in the future. If only we could remain in the moment, free of past messages and future fears, our vision would clear, we could see the people around us more accurately, and cases of mistaken identity no longer would weaken our ability to treat others with the respect and dignity they deserve. My father learned this, perhaps too late to help him live a better life, but not too late to teach his children an important lesson. His revelation came during the final weeks of his life as he lay dying in a Los Angeles hospital. Somehow the subject of bias came up—I have a vague memory that it had something to do with the black man who daily swept the hall outside my father's room—and my father turned to me and admitted that he had been wrong all his life. "People are people," he said, "We have to take 'em all just one person at a time."

Reducing bias is more than just taking one person at a time, however, it is also having the patience to take one step at a time in our efforts to resolve a monumental problem. As we saw earlier, many believe that fighting bias is a losing proposition. One reason for this pessimism is that the task seems overwhelming—as if we need to tackle and succeed with every hateful person we meet or are obligated to take a dramatic stance that will change the attitudes of a large number of people. In truth, our only obligation, and our only hope, is to commit to making one small gesture after one small gesture after one small gesture. None of us can follow Rosa Parks to that seat at the front of the bus and few have the opportunity to defy the philosophy of an era by reaching out to a lonely stranger like Dennis did to Tony. The small battles, the modest displays of courage, the day-to-day gestures of respect are, however, available to us all.

I witnessed one such gesture at a diversity workshop when a young woman refused to let the program adjourn until she was given the opportunity to stand up and say to the group, "It is time we begin to forgive." We glimpse another in Yoko's willingness to defend openly her male colleague against charges of sexism despite pressure to presume him guilty until proven innocent. Another equally elegant act of commitment was seen in the simple gesture of the father who attended a garage sale held by my family some years ago in Los Angeles. As part of an effort to rid ourselves of an obscene excess of material possessions, we had given the man's little girl one of the dozens of scarcely touched stuffed animals that my now-grown daughter had begged for on so many occasions. As the child, who was from Mexico, walked away, she uttered a barely audible "*Gracias,*" to which the father responded, in an obvious effort to communicate respect for a stranger, "No, say 'thank you.'"

The practice of every technique in this book would benefit from just this type of ability to attack bias in small well-crafted steps and to live life and its challenges one moment at a time. What better way to achieve the empathy discussed in "Identify Common Kinship Groups" than to stay present, in the moment, with the person whom you are trying to understand? What more effective posture could there be for resisting the urge to be offended than to push from your mind a history, however sad, of past abuses? How possibly could we be better able to listen effectively when in the middle of a gateway event than by shoving all other thoughts out of our minds? Finally, how better to be aware of our biased thoughts than by staying in the moment and clearing our flypaper brains of the bits and pieces and shards of the past that we insist on bringing to bear on current relationships?

Like shoving biases aside, being in the moment is a habit. I know it's a habit because most of us have been habituated to the opposite behavior since childhood. For years, we have allowed, and even encouraged, our minds to jump from subject to subject and from past to present to future. It is time we work to break that habit and focus on the now and on the individual before us. It is time we see people for who they are.

R *e a d e r* '*s* **G** *u i d e*

This Reader's Guide consists of brief summaries of each chapter followed by questions designed to encourage further dialogue and thought. The guide serves two functions. First, it allows readers to review what they have read and thus enhances the learning process. Second, it enables facilitators of diversity and bias-reduction workshops to foster in-depth discussions of the causes and cures of bias.

Part One: The Basics of Bias

Chapter 1: Bias Defined and Misdefined

Chapter Summary

A bias is an inflexible belief about a particular category (kinship group) of people. There are many misunderstandings about what bias is. An action, for example, cannot be biased; only attitudes are biased. Furthermore, a given action or thought may or may not be proof of or reflect a biased attitude. For example, being drawn to someone like oneself, mistaking one member of an unfamiliar group for another, and making a reasonable assumption about someone in light of current evidence are not necessarily evidence of bias. Just as some actions and attitudes are mistaken as bias, others, what are called Guerilla Biases, are overlooked. Like guerilla warriors who lie concealed behind beautiful trees, these biases are hidden behind what appear to be positive actions. Based on the premise that emerging group members are fragile and need special treatment, this kind of bias can be manifested in actions such as failing to coach an employee who needs improvement, holding emerging group members to a low standard of performance, or making unreasonable accommodations for cultural or ethnic differences.

Dialogue Questions

1. Do you agree with the distinction between a reasonable assumption and a bias as described in this chapter? Can you think of examples from your life or workplace in which a reasonable assumption was mistaken as a bias or vice versa?

2. This chapter lists several behaviors and argues that they do not necessarily reflect biased attitudes. Do you agree with this argument? If not, why not?

3. Much Guerilla Bias grows out of the premise that members of emerging groups are too fragile to survive the everyday wear and tear of slightly unfair situations, reasonable reprimands, or less-than-perfect language. Do you know anyone, including yourself, who believes that emerging group members really are this way? What consequences might this attitude have for your workplace?

4. Do you agree with the premise that holding people to a low standard of performance and behavior reflects a bias? If so, what are the consequences of this attitude in the workplace? If you do not agree, why not?

5. Discuss the pros and cons of politically correct language. What are the advantages of adhering to these rules? What are the liabilities?

Chapter 2: Carefully Taught: How Bias Is Learned

Chapter Summary

The reason we are so receptive to learning biases is that they provide us with the illusion that we can predict the characteristics and behaviors of people who are different from ourselves. Biases are learned from our parents (our "tribal leaders"), from the media, and from positive and negative experiences. Although blatant messages of bias are dangerous, the subtle and ambiguous ones are often the most difficult to resist and to cure. This is because they can be almost impossible to identify.

Once biases are learned, the culture as a whole plays a role in helping them thrive. This is particularly true of those cultures in which biased attitudes are tolerated. Because toleration perpetuates bias, it is important that these attitudes be corrected no matter who holds them. Individuals, too, are responsible for the survival of bias. Each of us, once we have acquired a prejudice, will distort external reality to reinforce what we believe. To make matters worse, the more firmly we believe a bias to be true, the more firmly we believe it to be good and desirable.

Dialogue Questions

1. One way in which we learn biases is through negative experiences. In addition to the reasons discussed in this chapter, why else might a negative experience result in a bias?
2. This chapter argues that biases cannot be tolerated regardless of who holds them. Do you agree with this view? If so, why? If not, why not?
3. This chapter argues that one reason we cling to biases is that we like the drama of feeling that we live in a dangerous world. How do you feel about this premise and what might be done to counter this attitude? Why else do human beings hang on to their biases?
4. What strategies might be employed in the workplace to prevent forming new biases?

Part Two: The Vision Renewal Process

Chapter 3: Step One—Become Mindful of Your Biases

Chapter Summary:

If we are to minimize our biases, we must, of course, become aware of their existence. Most of us resist admitting, even to ourselves, that we are biased. The reason for this resistance is the misguided belief that having a bias means we are no longer good people. This chapter argues that having a bias does not necessarily mean a person is bad; it means, instead, that he or she is trying to feel more secure in a complex and diverse world.

We need to become mindful of our biases so that we can systematically attack them with the goal of minimizing their negative impact on our ability to see people accurately. The process of bias awareness and diagnosis consists of three steps: Watching a thought that comes to mind in response to a kinship group; examining the logic of that thought; and determining how much emotion is attached to that thought. If the thought is accompanied by emotion, it is more apt to fall into the category of a bias. Another way to identify a bias is to ascertain how much emphasis we put on the differences between kinship groups. Too much or too little concern with difference can be an indication of a biased attitude.

Dialogue Questions

1. Do you agree with the premise of this chapter that having a bias does not necessarily indicate something bad about the person's fundamental character? If you do not agree, what is your argument?
2. This chapter contends that it is possible to watch the thoughts that come into our minds. Do you agree? If not, why not?
3. This chapter talks about the importance of observing your emotions when establishing the presence or absence of a bias. Do you agree that most biased attitudes are accompanied by some emotion? If so, what might some of these emotions be?
4. How might the notion of too much or too little attention to differences impact relationships in the workplace? What strategies might be employed in the workplace to balance these attitudes?
5. As a manager, what might you do to help others in the workplace become aware of their biases?

Chapter 4: Step Two—Identify the Alleged Benefits of Your Biases

Chapter Summary

One reason we cling to our biases is that they do, in fact, benefit us in several ways. To defeat our biases, we need to identify what those secondary gains are and weigh them against the damage the biases cause. These benefits are in some cases temporary and in others greatly exaggerated, but they still have an impact on our lives. They include: the relief of guilt for having treated a population poorly; protection from loss of status; protection from loss of livelihood or, ultimately, life; protection from the repetition of emotional pain; and protection of community or individual values. Biases also provide us with an excuse to stay away from those around whom we are uncomfortable.

Dialogue Questions

1. This chapter lists several functions that biases allegedly serve. Can you add to this list?

2. This chapter talks about a particular type of bias called the *bias bias*. Do you believe there is such a thing? If so, why? If not, why not?

3. What argument can you make that the benefits of bias listed in this chapter are not really benefits after all?

Chapter 5: Step Three—Put Your Biases through Triage

Chapter Summary

To identify which biases we should attack first, we need to balance the benefits outlined in Chapter 4 against the ways in which the bias interferes with our ability to function effectively in the workplace. Biases compromise effectiveness in many areas, including hiring and retention, productivity, building diverse teams, and sales. They can also give rise to litigation, not only in cases of blatant discrimination, but also through subtler biases that prevent us from coaching employees properly and delivering appropriate service to customers of all backgrounds.

Dialogue Questions

1. This chapter lists several ways in which biases interfere with functioning in the workplace. Can you think of any that are not included?

2. This chapter contains a discussion of how bias can interfere with employee retention. Discuss this issue and include strategies for overcoming these difficulties.

3. Hector's career has been adversely affected by his managers' biases. Discuss Hector's situation. Do you agree that it was a bias that created his difficulties? If you disagree, why? If you agree, what other options did management have when expanding its business into a Latino neighborhood?

4. Propose some ways that managers can distinguish between appropriate adjustments for cultural differences and the kind of excessive accommodation that can compromise the effectiveness of the team.

Chapter 6: Step Four—Dissect Your Biases

Chapter Summary

One of the most important steps in the Vision Renewal Process is to subject each of our biases to a strict test of logic. This means, first, to examine how we learned each bias to reveal its weak foundation and faulty beginnings. Was the source reliable? The initiating experience, for example, might have been distorted by the emotions we brought to the situation. We also need to question how much actual experience we have had with the group in question and explore whether or not we have had encounters with individuals who do not conform to our bias. The second component of the dissection process is to increase our knowledge of the group and expose ourselves to as wide a variety of people as possible.

Dialogue Questions

1. This chapter talks about how our initial experiences with members of other groups can be distorted by the emotions we bring to the encounter. What other factors might distort these experiences and our memory of them? How can we prevent this distortion from taking place?
2. Do you agree with Emerson that "Knowledge is the antidote to fear"? If so, what strategies involving knowledge might you employ to minimize bias in your workplace?
3. How can we keep the knowledge gained about various kinship groups from degenerating into new biases and stereotypes?
4. How might you change the mind of someone who says his bias (his "inflexible belief") is true because every person he has ever met conforms to what he believes?

Chapter 7: Step Five—Identify Common Kinship Groups

Chapter Summary

If we are to minimize bias, we need to broaden and multiply our notion of the kinship groups to which we belong so we can redefine who is "them" and who is "us." This means, in essence, to focus less on the ways in which we differ and more on what we share. There are several ways to do this. These include recognizing that "race," although certainly a powerful force in society, is not a physiological reality. We can also multiply our kinship groups by using the "Magic If" technique to empathize and, therefore, identify with the experiences of others. The Magic If is particularly valuable in helping members of the so-called majority empathize with what it is like to be the object of bias. Kinship groups can also be expanded by identifying shared values and developing common goals.

Dialogue Questions

1. This chapter talks about multiplying and broadening our kinship groups to expand the notion of "like me." In what ways, other than those mentioned, might this be accomplished?
2. Do you agree with the premise of the Magic If? If so, how might this doctrine be applied in the workplace to improve the functioning of diverse teams?
3. The chapter argues that it is possible for anyone to empathize with the pain suffered by emerging groups. Do you agree with this statement? If not, why not?
4. What processes might your workplace put in place to encourage the identification of shared values, common human experience, and expanded kinship groups?

Chapter 8: Step Six—Shove Your Biases Aside

Chapter Summary

Once we are aware of our biases, have questioned their logic, and have attempted to broaden our own group to include others, we are prepared for the next step: shoving our biases aside so we can see people more accurately. This is a mechanical act that, if practiced regularly, becomes a habit. As each bias is pushed out of the way, we are able to see people accurately and, therefore, relate to them more appropriately. Experiences will gradually accumulate in which we view members of a particular group as unique individuals and, as a result, our biases—our inflexible generalities—begin to fade.

Dialogue Questions

1. This chapter talks of how the previous steps have prepared the reader for the process of shoving biases aside. What other preparation might make this practice easier?

2. The practice of shoving a thought aside seems difficult to some people. How might you help others in your workplace better understand and execute this concept?

Chapter 9: Step Seven—Beware the Bias Revival

Chapter Summary

Even when we believe we have defeated a bias, it can come back to life. The reason these "revivals" occur so easily is that we receive secondary gains from our biases and don't really want to let them go. Relapses happen, for example, when we meet someone who conforms to our bias. When this occurs, we must remind ourselves that one person is never representative of the entire group. Biases can also reappear in response to dramatic public events like terrorist attacks or discrimination suits. In cases like these, it is important to make sure that the details of what happened are accurately and thoroughly reported.

In the unlikely event that a bias cannot be defeated, it can be helpful to "fake it till you make it," to treat people as if the bias does not exist. The principle of cognitive dissonance dictates that attitudes will follow behavior and the very act of treating people with respect can extinguish a biased attitude.

Dialogue Questions

1. This chapter discusses the danger of a long dormant bias coming back to life. How might we guard against this happening and how might we remedy the situation if it does occur?
2. Do you agree that "faking it till you make it" can help diminish a biased attitude? If so, how might this strategy be encouraged in the workplace?
3. In the event of a well-publicized workplace event that might be a catalyst for renewed biases, what might you do as a manager to minimize the impact?

Part Three: Gateway Events: Entering into Diversity Dialogue

Chapter 10: The Benefits of Diversity Dialogue

Chapter Summary

Although entering into conversations about bias can be challenging and frightening, the benefits far outweigh the risks. More than anything else, such conversations serve an important educational function. Not only do they allow us to share our points of view and cultural perspectives, they provide an opportunity to educate others about appropriate and inappropriate behaviors. Conversation also diminishes the destructive impact of rumor and minimizes the spread of bias by making it clear that such attitudes are unacceptable.

Dialogue Questions

1. Several benefits of talking about bias are mentioned in this chapter. Can you think of any that ought to be added to this discussion?
2. Can you think of any disadvantages to having conversations about bias? If so, under what circumstances should such conversations be avoided?
3. What facilities or arrangements might be made in your workplace to encourage people to honestly discuss the issues of bias and diversity?

Chapter 11: Getting Diversity Fit

Chapter Summary

Becoming diversity fit is a way of preparing ourselves for the unexpected gateway events that come our way. This fitness regimen involves identifying and thus controlling the fears that cause us to function poorly during such conversations. These emotions prevent us from thinking clearly, interfere with our ability to interpret accurately what is going on, and make it difficult to focus on present reality rather than on past events. The particular fear that causes all these problems may be fear of intimacy, fear of our own biases showing, fear of the other person's anger, or simply fear of being judged.

Dialogue Questions

1. This chapter discusses several fears that tend to come upon us in the face of gateway events. Are there any others that you have experienced that were not mentioned here?
2. This chapter states that identifying the fears that interfere with effective diversity dialogue is an important strategy for minimizing their influence. What other steps might you propose for getting our fears under control?

Chapter 12: Cognitive Skills for Diversity Dialogue

Chapter Summary

Dialogue about bias requires certain cognitive skills if our conversations are to be successful. These skills include stopping to think before jumping to conclusions regarding the significance of a gateway event and identifying what we want to accomplish in a conversation before proceeding. Also, it is imperative that we look for, and admit to, the mutual contributions that all participants make to any diversity conflict. This does not mean that all, or even any, of the contributors are wrong, but merely that their actions in some way have played a role in bringing the event about. The ability to recognize a common enemy is another skill that can greatly enhance the productivity of our conversations. In all cases, that enemy is the bias that permeates our culture and affects us all in many ways. Finally, there are times when we need to adopt a Pyramid Strategy in which we build a foundation of small successes—one stone at a time—before tackling the larger issue that is creating the conflict.

Dialogue Questions

1. This chapter recounts several gateway events involving different personalities. Pick one and discuss how the event was handled. Do you agree with what the parties did? If not, what might they have done differently?
2. It is important to set goals before entering into diversity dialogue. What goals might you add to those listed in this chapter?
3. This chapter mentions the importance of recognizing that bias is a common enemy that we all share. Do you agree with this notion? If not, why not?

4. Discuss the section "Recognize Mutual Contributions" in terms of other ways in which individuals might contribute to a conflict around bias. What strategies might be implemented in the workplace to identify and minimize these contributions?

Chapter 13: Verbal Skills for Diversity Dialogue

Chapter Summary

Because of the delicate and often emotional nature of diversity dialogue, it is important that we learn to modulate both our tone of voice and our choice of words when having these conversations. This means to avoid exaggerated labels and absolute statements that can end a conversation before it has had a chance to begin. It is also important that we resist the temptation to respond to crude or disrespectful language in a way that lowers ourselves to the other person's level. Good listening skills and creative communication that takes the other person's background and experience into consideration are also key to success when dialoguing about diversity.

Dialogue Questions

1. In addition to the suggestions in this chapter, what other ideas do you have about how we can use language more effectively when talking about bias?
2. This chapter emphasizes the importance of softening both tone and choice of words when engaged in a gateway event. Do you agree with this strategy? Are there times when this approach is not the most effective?
3. Why is listening so important in good communication? What benefits does listening provide? Why is it sometimes so difficult to listen effectively?
4. What programs or strategies might you develop to increase the ability of your workforce to dialogue effectively about diversity?

Endnotes

Introduction

1. Patti Hanson, "Why Employees Leave: The Root Cause of Employee Departure," retrieved 10 January 2003 from <www.shrm.org>.

2. Kipp Cheng, "New Numbers Make the Case: Ethnic Spending Power Continues Rapid Rise," retrieved 10 January 2003 from <www.diversityinc.com>.

3. "Finally, the Truth: How Many Gay Americans Are There and What Will They Buy?," *DiversityInc.* (Nov./Dec. 2002), 65.

4. Edward E. Hubbard, "Measuring Diversity Results Series—Article 1," *Profiles in Diversity Journal* (March/April 2002).

5. Bruce Jacobs, *Race Manners* (New York: Arcade Publishing, 1999), 50.

Chapter One

1. Joseph Ponterotti and Paul Pedersen, *Preventing Prejudice* (Newbury Park: Sage Publications, 1993), 52.

2. Nathaniel Branden, *The Six Pillars of Self-Esteem* (New York: Bantam, 1994), 43.

3. Indra Lahiri, "Avoid Bloopers in Multicultural Marketing," *Cultural Diversity at Work* (May 1999).

4. *San Diego Union-Tribune* (15 July 1993).

Chapter Two

1. Gordon Allport, *The Nature of Prejudice* (New York: Addison-Wesley Publishing Company, 1979), 9.

2. *The Nature of Prejudice*, 22.

3. Paul Wachtel, *Race in the Mind of America* (New York: Routledge, 1999), 109.

4. Jennifer James, *Thinking in the Future Tense* (New York: Simon and Schuster, 1997), 155.

5. Daryl Bem, *Beliefs, Attitudes, and Human Affairs* (Belmont, California: Brooks/Cole Publishing Company, 1970), 43–44.

6. *Beliefs, Attitudes, and Human Affairs*, 27.

Chapter Three

1. Jim Adamson, *The Denny's Story* (New York: John Wiley & Sons, Inc., 2000), 66.

Chapter Four

1. Carl Hovland and Robert Sears, "Minor Studies of Aggression: Correlation of Lynchings With Economic Indices," *Journal of Psychology* (1940).

Chapter Five

1. David Shipler, "Seeing Through," *The Washington Post* (4 May 1997).

Chapter Six

1. Jennifer James, *Thinking in the Future Tense: A Workout for the Mind* (New York: Touchstone, 1996), 220.

2. Ralph Waldo Emerson, "Society of Solitude," *Courage* (1870).

3. Population Reference Bureau, 1996.

4. Latino National Political Survey, 1992.

5. "Taking America's Pulse: The National Conference Survey on Inter-Group Relations," *The National Conference* (n.d.), 10.

Chapter Seven

1. Paul Wachtel, *Race in the Mind of America* (New York: Routledge, 1999), 134.

2. John Dovidio, "The Subtlety of Racism," *Training and Development* (April 1993), 51–57.

3. James Baldwin and Margaret Mead, *A Rap on Race* (New York: Del Publishing, 1971), 25–26.

4. Tom Morganthau, "What Color is Black?," *Newsweek* (13 February 1995), 68.

5. Paul R. Ehrlich, *Human Natures: Genes, Cultures, and the Human Prospect* (Washington, D.C.: Island Press, 2000), 49.

6. Robert Lee Hotz, "Is Concept of Race a Relic," *Los Angeles Times* (15 April 1995).

7. *Human Natures: Genes, Cultures, and the Human Prospect,* 8.

8. Rosie Mestel, "Tiny Disparities in Human Genes Go a Long Way, Studies Find," *Los Angeles Times* (12 February 2001).

9. Sharon Begley, "Three is Not Enough," *Newsweek* (13 February 1995).

10. Colin Powell with Joseph E. Persico, *My American Journey* (New York: Random House, 1995), 107–108.

11. George Harris, *Dignity and Vulnerability: Strength and Quality of Character* (Berkeley: University of California Press, 1997).

12. Translation: If any of you are Swedish, you are capable of reading this paragraph. For those who aren't, this passage will serve as a jolt of what it feels like to be disoriented, left out, and confused about what is happening. These words were translated into Swedish by my dear father-in-law, Dr. Åke Sandler. Although I trust Åke to do a great job, it is still somewhat disconcerting to have a passage in my book that I cannot read. In that sense, this devise served to teach me too what it is like to be just a little bit out of control.

Chapter Nine

1. Daryl J. Bem, *Beliefs, Attitudes and Human Affairs* (Belmont, California: Brooks/Cole Publishing Company, 1970), 54.

2. *Beliefs, Attitudes and Human Affairs,* 55ff.

3. Jennifer James, *Thinking in the Future Tense: A Workout for the Mind* (New York: Touchstone, 1997), 78–79.

Part Three

1. Bruce Jacobs, *Race Manners: Navigating the Minefield Between Black and White Americans* (New York: Arcade Publishing, 1999), 1.

2. *Race Manners,* 155.

Chapter Eleven

1. Bruce Jacobs, *Race Manners* (New York: Arcade Publishing, 1999), 11.

Chapter Twelve

1. Douglas Stone, Bruce Patton, Sheila Heen, *Difficult Conversations: How to Discuss What Matters Most* (New York: Penguin Books, 1999), 46–50.

2. Solomon Moore, "Expressions of Support Surprising to Muslims," *Los Angeles Times* (26 September 2001).

3. Roosevelt Thomas, *Building a House for Diversity* (New York: AMA-COM, 1999), 61.

Chapter Thirteen

1. Roger Kahn, "A Tribute to Captain Courageous," *Los Angeles Times* (19 August 1999).

2. Paul Wachtel, *Race in the Mind of America* (New York: Routledge, 1999), 37.

3. Douglas Stone, Bruce Patton, Sheila Heen, *Difficult Conversations: How to Discuss What Matters Most* (New York: Penguin Books, 1999), 13.

Index

A

Ackerman, Roger, 79, 111–12
Acquisition, of bias, 7, 35–44,
    180–81
    belief perseverance, 43–44
    culture and, 41–42
    experiences and, 39–41, 88–91,
        122–23
    home atmosphere and, 38–39,
        88
    media and, 42–43, 88
Adamson, Jim, 58, 112
Advantages, perceived, 108–9
Adventure of the Empty House, The
    (Doyle), 119
Aleem, Mohammed Abdul, 152–53
Allport, Gordon, 38, 40
Anger, fear of, 144
Arab-Americans, 63–64
Aristotle, 124
Asian-American consumers, 2
Assumptions, 25–26, 32–33
Attitude(s)
    behavior and, 123–24
    biased, 21, 32
    examination of, 47–60
    faking it, 125–27
Awareness, 49–61, 181–82
    analyzing your thoughts, 54–56
    attitude examination, 57–60
    identifying biases, 50–51, 182
    measuring emotional content,
        56–57, 61, 94
    observing your thoughts,
        51–54

B

Behavior
    as evidence of bias, 51, 61
    attempts to predict, 36–37, 44,
        64
    excuses for, 68–70
    perception of discrimination
        and, 125
Belief perseverance, 43–44
Bem, Daryl, 42, 124
Benedict, Ruth, 97–98
Bias(es)
    accusations of, 155–57
    acquisition of. *See* Acquisition,
        of bias
    alleged benefits of, 63–72
    attacking harmful, 73–74
    awareness of. *See* Awareness
    bias bias, 67–68
    defined, 1, 8, 19, 21, 32, 46, 179
    dissection of, 87–94
    examining, 13
    function/benefit of, 61
    Guerilla Bias, 26–31, 72, 179
    misdefinition of, 21–26, 179
    price of, 1–3
    revival of, 119–27, 186
Branden, Nathaniel, 23
Buchanan, Singer, 92

C

Canine Companions for
    Independence, 112
Ceconi, Barbara, 75, 154

Chen, Zhao Lin, 109
Childhood experiences, and bias,
    39–40, 88
Coca-Cola, 2
Cognitive dissonance, 124
Cognitive skills, 147–64, 188
    goal identification, 152–58
    Pyramid Strategy and, 163–64
    recognizing a common enemy,
        158–59
    recognizing mutual
        contributions, 159–62
    resist/remember/rethink,
        148–52
Common enemies, recognizing,
    158–59
Communication
    creative, 170–71
    styles, 161–62
    terms of art, 8–10
Community values, alleged
    protection of, 70–71, 72
Contributions, recognizing mutual,
    159–62
Coping, 50
Cross talk, 172
Cultural acceptance, 22–23
Cultural characteristics, 82
Culture, and bias, 41–42
cummings, e.e., 31

D

Danger, stimulation of, 41, 44
Decision makers, determining
    identity of, 82
Defensiveness, 64–65, 148–49
Devalued achievements, 108–9
Diamond, Jared, 99
Differences
    denial of, 58–59
    examining attitudes about,
        57–60
    excessive awareness of, 60
Difficult Conversations (Stone, Patton,
    and Heen), 149, 172
Discrimination suits, 2
Dishonesty, 1

Diversity dialogue, 7–8
    benefits of, 133–39, 187
    cognitive skills for, 147–64, 188.
        See also Cognitive skills
    fear and, 142–45
    increased knowledge/
        understanding and, 134–36
    rumor reduction and, 136–38
    stifling spread of bias with,
        138–39
    verbal skills for, 165–74, 189
Dogmatic language, 168–69, 173
Dostoyevsky, Fyodor, 49
Doyle, Arthur Conan, 119

E

Emerging groups, 9–10, 105–7
Emerson, Ralph Waldo, 92
Emotion
    acknowledging shared, 100–109
    as measure of bias, 56–57, 61
    distortion and, 89–90, 94, 184
    hyperbole and, 168
    protection from emotional
        pain, 67–68, 72
    resisting venting of, 149
Emotional intelligence, 142
Empathy, 100–103
Employees
    hiring, 74–76, 86
    losing, cost of, 2
    retaining quality, 76–78, 86
Employment Practices Liability
    insurance, 2
Ethnic identity, 22–23
Experiences, and bias, 39–41, 44,
    88–91, 122–23
Exploration Points
    attitudes toward differences, 97
    cognitive dissonance, 124
    discussing race issue, 143
    dissection of biases, 88, 94
    diversity dialogues, 144
    emotional pain, protection
        from, 68
    empathy, 104, 107
    faking nonbiased attitude, 126

goals, 155, 156
Guerilla Bias, 30
harmonious teams, 81
hiring decisions, 76
kinship groups, 53, 57, 111, 114
litigation potential, 85
minimizing contact, 70
noticing human differences, 58
parental messages, 39
positive biases, 31
protection from loss, 67, 72
protection of values, 71
relief of guilt, 65, 72
resist, remember, and rethink,
    152
retaining quality employees,
    78
self-esteem, 23
self-fulfilling prophecies, 79
societal status, 66, 72
unnecessary mention of
    differences, 60
verbal skills, 168, 169, 170
Exposure, to differences, 92–93

F

Fear, 37, 49, 142, 143–44, 145
    conversation as weapon of, 130
Flexibility *vs.* inflexibility, 21, 32
Footlocker Specialty, 2
Freud, Sigmund, 100

G

Gateway events, 130–31. *See also*
    Cognitive skills; Verbal skills
Generalities, 44, 67
Goals
    identifying, 152–58
    shared, 110–12
Group self-esteem, 23–24
Guerilla Bias, 26–31, 33, 51, 68–69,
    72, 80
    "noble savage," 29–31
    defined, 26–28
    holding people to low standard
        of excellence, 29

parents and, 38
political overcorrectness, 28–29
Guilt feelings, 64–65, 72

H

Hanamura, Steve, 75, 76, 104
Harris, George, 102
Harvard Negotiation Project, 149
Heen, Sheila, 149
Home atmosphere, and bias, 38–39
Homophobia, 167
Honesty, 143
Hovland, Carl, 66
Hubbard, Edward, 3
Human differences, examining
    attitudes toward, 57–60
Humanity, shared, 112–14
Hyperbole, 167

I

Identity confusion, 103–4
Individual values, alleged protection
    of, 70–71, 72
Inflexible generalities, 67
Intimacy, fear of, 143
Izell, Booker, 171–72

J

Jacobs, Bruce, 14, 130, 143
James, Jennifer, 41, 87, 124
James, William, 37
Johnson, Samuel, 3

K

Kinship groups, 10, 22–24, 32, 184
    exploration points, 53, 57, 111,
        114
    objective knowledge of, 93–94
    personal contact with different,
        92–93
    redefining, 95–114
    shared goals, 110–12
    shared humanity, 112–14
    shared work ethic, 109–10, 114

Kinship groups, *continued*
    sharing, and bias reduction,
        96–98
Kuss, Kurt, 75, 76

L

Language barriers, 82, 107
Listening skills, 171–73, 174
Litigation, 2, 84–85, 86
Loss, protection from, 66–67, 72
Low expectations, 29

M

*Man's Most Dangerous Myth: The
    Fallacy of Race* (Montagu), 98
Mead, Margaret, 98
Media, 41, 42–43
Minority
    as descriptive term, 9
    feeling part of a, 105–7
Modulation, 166–68, 173
Montagu, Ashley, 98
Morality, 12
Murrow, Edward R., 45

N–O

Negotiation strategies, 82
Noble savage doctrine, 29, 65
Notes from the Underground
    (Dostoyevsky), 49
Oppressed, as descriptive term, 9

P

Parents, and bias, 38–39, 44, 88
Parks, Rosa, 176
Patton, Bruce, 149
Pavlov's dogs, 138
Pedersen, Paul, 22, 23
People of color, as descriptive term, 9
Perceptions, distorted, 30
Personal contact, 92–93
Personal fictions, 4, 50
Personal self-esteem, 23

Phillips, Ray Hood, 58
Physical disabilities, 75–76
Political overcorrectness, 28–29
Polk, Tony, 16, 129, 137–38
Ponterotti, Joseph, 22, 23
Powell, Colin, 99–100
Preparedness, 142–45
Productivity, 79–80, 86
Public speaking, 22
Pyramid Strategy, 163–64

R

Race, acknowledging a shared,
    98–100
Race in the Mind of America
    (Wachtel), 167
Race Manners (Jacobs), 14, 130
Racial bias, 5–6, 8, 11
Racial profiling, 29
Recruitment costs, 2
Reese, PeeWee, 165–66
Remembering, 150–51
Resisting, 148–50
Rethinking, 151–52
Robinson, Jackie, 165–66
Rousseau, Jean-Jacques, 29
Rumors, 136–38

S

Sales, 2, 81–83, 86
Sears, Robert, 66
Self-esteem, 23
Self-fulfilling prophecies, 79
Semantic generalization, 42
September 11 terrorist attack,
    63–64, 122, 152–53
Sexism, 6, 8
Simpson, O.J., trial of, 133–34, 139
Stanislavsky, Constantin, 100
State Farm Insurance, 2
Status, protection against
    diminished, 65–66, 72
Stereotypes, 30–31
Stone, Douglas, 149
Superstitions, 37

T

Tacitus, 64
Terms of art, 8–10
Terror management theory, 40–41
Terrorist attack of September 11,
    63–64, 122, 152–53
Texaco, 2
Thomas, Roosevelt, 153
Time, wasted, 3

U–V

Understatement, 167
Values, alleged protection of, 70–71,
    72
Verbal skills, 165–74
    creative communication,
        170–71
    dogmatic language, avoiding,
        168–69
    listening and, 171–73
        maintaining high standards,
            170, 173
        verbal/vocal modulation,
            166–68
Vision Renewal Process, 7, 45–47

W–Z

Wachtel, Paul, 167
Work ethic, 109–10, 114
Workplace biases, 73–86, 183
    corporate productivity and,
        79–80
    hiring employees and, 74–76
    litigation risk and, 84–85
    retaining quality employees
        and, 76–78
    sales efforts and, 81–83
    teamwork and, 80–81
World Trade Center attack, 63–64,
    122, 152–53
Zero-order belief, 89